STRESS
ALL THAT MATTERS

About the author

Michael Hyland is Professor of Health Psychology at Plymouth University where he teaches psychology. He is a Chartered Health Psychologist and Fellow of the British Psychological Society and a Distinguished International Affiliate of the Health Psychology Division of the American Psychological Association. In addition to research papers and books, he has published one textbook for psychology undergraduates and two for health professionals.

STRESS

Michael E. Hyland

ALL THAT MATTERS

First published in Great Britain in 2014 by John Murray Learning. An Hachette UK company.

First published in US in 2014 by The McGraw-Hill Companies, Inc.

This edition published in 2014 by John Murray Learning

British Library Cataloguing in Publication Data: a catalogue record for this title is available from the British Library.

Library of Congress Catalog Card Number: on file.

Paperback ISBN 978 1 471 80160 0

eBook ISBN 978 1 471 80567 7

10 9 8 7 6 5 4 3 2 1

The publisher has used its best endeavours to ensure that any website addresses referred to in this book are correct and active at the time of going to press. However, the publisher and the author have no responsibility for the websites and can make no guarantee that a site will remain live or that the content will remain relevant, decent or appropriate.

The publisher has made every effort to mark as such all words which it believes to be trademarks. The publisher should also like to make it clear that the presence of a word in the book, whether marked or unmarked, in no way affects its legal status as a trademark.

Every reasonable effort has been made by the publisher to trace the copyright holders of material in this book. Any errors or omissions should be notified in writing to the publisher, who will endeavour to rectify the situation for any reprints and future editions.

Typeset by Cenveo® Publisher

Printed and bound in Great Br

John Murray Learning policy i
recyclable products and made
and manufacturing processes
regulations of the country of c

John Murray Learning

338 Euston Road

London NW1 3BH

www.hodder.co.uk

Contents

What is stress?

'The meaning of a word is to be defined by the rules for its use, not by the feeling that attaches to the words.'

Ludwig Wittgenstein, philosopher (1889–1951)

The word 'stress' is used in three different senses. First, 'stress' is used in the sense of a state – that is, the state of being stressed. People say, 'I am feeling stressed.' The state of stress is commonly referred to as a *stress response* or *stress reaction.* The second meaning of stress is the thing that is causing the stress response. People say, 'My work is a real stress at the moment.' The thing causing stress is commonly referred to as a *stressor.* Finally, the term 'stress' can also be used in the sense of a combination of a stressor and a stress response. For example, it is possible to refer to 'the stress of modern life', where the meaning of stress refers both to the stressors and their consequent stress response.

Although the word 'stress' is used in everyday language, there are four differences between its use in common language and the way 'stress' is used in science.

First, stressors do not have to be aversive or unpleasant. Weddings can produce stress responses (at least for the bride) and so does marathon running. People choose to have weddings and they choose to run marathons. A whole range of happy events can act as stressors. People can choose to act in ways that create stress responses.

Second, it is incorrect to understand stress as being something that is 'only' psychological and so unimportant. Phrases such as 'Oh, it's just stress' or 'It's just a stress-related illness' indicate a dismissal of stress as something without serious consequences. In fact, the stress response is *always* physiological as well as psychological. These responses are not separate. The psychological response is *the consequence* of the physiological response. Minds do not occur without bodies! The link between physiological state and psychological state is increasingly well understood, so the psychological response needs to be interpreted in the context of the underlying physiology.

Third, the response to stressors is highly variable, both between people and for the same person over time. One of the first stress researchers, Hans Selye, suggested that the effect of a stressor changed over time. At first there was an *alarm reaction*. Then there was an *adaptation stage*. Finally, there was a *stage of exhaustion*. While Selye's three stages are now considered simplistic, the reality is that the response to a stressor *does* change over time. Although the changes aren't as neat as Selye suggested, certain changes do take place at different stages. Additionally, the changes that occur in people exposed to the same stressor will vary between individuals.

Fourth, stress responses are not necessarily 'bad'. The human body is designed to cope with all kinds of adverse event. The human body adapts to good events and bad events. Humans evolved to perform dangerous – and hence stressful – activities such as hunting mammoths. But humans did not evolve to hunt mammoths all the time. Stressors typically cause problems only when the stressor persists for a long time. The difference between short-term and long-term, or chronic, stress is therefore important. Short-term stress is stress that is over and done with in less than a day. Long-term stress is stress that goes on, day after day. Short-term stress produces short-term changes that revert back to normal once the stressor has gone. Long-term stress produces long-term changes that persist. However, it is not quite that simple. Very traumatic short-term stress produces long-term changes.

This book describes the nature of stressors, how they cause stress responses and the consequence of those stress responses. Stressors and stress responses are defined by each other: 'a stressor is that which causes a stress response.'

Although stressors are defined by stress responses, stressors are causally antecedent to stress responses, and so it makes sense to explore the nature of stressors before that of stress responses.

▶ How this book is organized

This book covers the following topics:

▶ **Chapter 2** provides an account of stressors, and specifically stressors that typically produce a stress response in most people. Stressors can be biological, psychological or some combination of the two.

▶ **Chapter 3** describes why some people vary in their level of stress response to a particular stressor. This chapter also deals with the topic of personality, as personality is one of the factors that affect a person's response to stress.

▶ **Chapter 4** provides an account of the short-term effects of stress, from both a biological and a psychological perspective. The chapter shows how the short-term stress response – that is, the fight-or-flight response – is highly adaptive.

▶ **Chapter 5** describes the long-term effects of stress, from both a biological and a psychological perspective, and shows how chronic stress produces long-term, persistent changes in people. The chapter shows how chronic stress affects people's behaviour.

▶ **Chapter 6** provides information about the way long-term stress creates disease and how almost all disease could be considered stress related. The chapter deals with the effects of biological stress in the womb, the effects of childhood abuse and neglect, and the effects of stressors in later life.

▶ **Chapter 7** is a chapter devoted to the measurement of stress and how it is possible to detect whether or not a person is stressed.

▶ **Chapter 8** covers the relationship between stress and society and how cultural values contribute to stress.

▶ **Chapter 9** deals with the flipside of the stress response, namely the relaxation response. The relaxation response is important for understanding how to deal with and minimize the effects of a stressor.

There is a simple message from this book. Humans are adapted to deal with short-term stress but not with chronic stress. Chronic stress (i.e., the stress response to a long-term stressor) is far more of a problem, in terms of both health and social problems, than is often realized.

What are stressors?

'Life is not always a matter of holding good cards, but sometimes, playing a poor hand well.'

Jack London, author (1876–1917)

It is normal to switch a car's engine on only when driving. It is uneconomical to park the car and then leave the engine running overnight. The body functions in a similar way: it is uneconomical to invest energy into doing things when they are not needed. The body needs to be able to react to emergencies but it does not need to be on permanent alert.

The body alters its environment adaptively except when asleep. Even when awake, bodies can be in a 'quiet' state of comparative inactivity. People, and their bodies, are designed to wake up and take notice of three classes of event:

▶ **Novel stimuli** – when something is new

▶ **Frustration** – when some desired goal cannot be reached

▶ **Punishment** – when an aversive state is experienced.

The response to any of these three classes of event is called an *alerting response*. The person becomes alert and pays attention to the stimulus. The alerting response is not exactly equivalent to a stress response, as the term 'stress response' is normally reserved for instances of comparatively high alert. The alerting response varies in intensity, depending on how much the body decides 'an alert' is needed. A stress response is one where there is moderate to high alert.

Acute versus chronic stressors

Novel, frustrating or punishing situations can occur over the short term or the long term. It is common to distinguish between acute and chronic stressors:

Acute stressors are stressors (whether experienced in a laboratory setting or in real life) of only a short duration.

Chronic stressors reflect ongoing and long-term problems in real life.

▶ Common stressors

The following table shows a list of common stressors. The list is taken from the Holmes and Rahe stress scale, an assessment scale that provides a list of 43 stressors. The ten most severe stressors are shown at the top and the ten least severe at the bottom. The Holmes and Rahe scale is sometimes used to assess the level of stress in a person's life. The numbers shown against each stressor are ratings of how stressful each situation was perceived to be by a group of judges, and a total score is obtained by a summation of those numbers.

Three observations can be made about the Holmes and Rahe scale:

1 The list of stressors is culturally determined.

2 Less severe stressors are often very minor events.

3 Stressors can be positive events.

▼ Part of the Holmes and Rahe stress scale

Life event	Value
Death of a spouse	100
Divorce	73
Marital separation	65
Imprisonment	63
Death of a close family member	63
Personal injury or illness	53
Marriage	50
Dismissal from work	47
Retirement	45
Marital reconciliation	45
...	
Change in recreation	19
Change in church activities	19
Change in social activities	18
Minor mortgage or loan	17
Change in sleeping habits	16
Change in number of family reunions	15
Change in eating habits	15
Vacation	13
Christmas	12
Minor violation of law	11

Stressors vary between cultures, and this variation is reflected in any list of stressors. For example, Christmas is listed as stressful because it involves entertaining family and friends, but similar festivals celebrated in other cultures can be just as stressful. Torture is comparatively uncommon in Western society, but torture can be just as or more stressful than the death of a spouse.

A good example of the cultural determination of stressors is illustrated in the term 'the stress of modern life' – a term that was used as early as 1905. Yes, modern life does have stressors that did not occur in 'ancient life' but that does not necessarily mean that ancient life was less stressful than modern life. Common ancient stressors would have included lack of food and ever-present physical danger. It is much safer to walk in a European or American street today than it was even 300 years ago, and death by starvation is now comparatively rare in Western societies – though both these stressors occur elsewhere in the world today.

The second point is that the minor stressors at the bottom of the scale merge into very minor stressors, which are sometimes referred to as *hassles*. Some research suggests that chronic hassles also have an effect on health and happiness.

A final point, and one referred to in the previous chapter, is that stressors can still be positive events. Anything that creates an alerting response, irrespective of whether it 'feels' positive or not, creates the physiological responses associated with stress. The equivalent of a positive hassle, which is a minor alerting but positive event, is called an *uplift*.

Despite its cultural specificity and despite the merging of stressors into hassles, the Holmes and Rahe scale provides a useful starting point for understanding the three causes of the alerting response: novelty, frustration and punishment.

▶ Novelty

Several events in the Holmes and Rahe list are stressful because of their novelty. Marriage is a novel event – at least to most people. Many of the less stressful events – such as change in eating habits and vacation – are stressful because of their novelty. Note that many of these minor stressors are normally considered positive events. Most people enjoy going on holiday; and getting married, which is one of the more stressful events, is something that people choose to do. The body is designed for novelty. It is designed for short-term stressors. Just because something is a stressor does not necessarily make it an unpleasant experience. On the contrary, novelty is often exciting, although it does create an alerting response.

One reason why novelty creates an alerting response is because novelty brings uncertainty. In uncertain times, the body prepares itself for any eventuality. That eventuality may require increased effort. So, if a holiday is full of uncertainty, then it is more likely to be experienced as stressful.

Uncertainty coupled with a possible positive outcome creates far less of an alerting response than uncertainty coupled with a possible negative outcome. Chronic and life-threatening illnesses are stressors, in part because of the uncertainty of exacerbations.

A novel situation does not create an alerting response if there are other cues that signal safety, indicating that there is no need for alarm. Going for a massage can be a relatively novel experience, but it is almost always experienced as relaxing. The key to understanding whether novelty will be a stressor is therefore the level of uncertainty. It is high levels of uncertainty, particularly when combined with threat, that are stressful. Low

Package holidays

Package holidays and guided tours are not popular with everyone, but they are certainly popular. One reason for their popularity is that they reduce uncertainty. The holidaymaker on a package tour is met by the 'tour representative' at the airport holding the sign of the company aloft. The holidaymaker is reassured. The holidaymaker knows that the holiday will bring novelty, but that any novelty is unlikely to be a hassle because the tour rep is always at hand to arrange things.

levels of uncertainty require only a minimal alerting response.

▶ Frustration

Many different kinds of need motivate human behaviour. A stressor is anything that prevents the satisfaction of an *important* need. Rather obviously, people usually don't get stressed if they can't have their favourite breakfast cereal. They get stressed only when important needs are not satisfied.

Humans have biological needs and they have psychological needs. Frustration of either kind of need can cause stress.

Biological need frustration

Biological needs include the need for food, the need for water, the need to keep a comfortable temperature, the need for sleep and the need for safety. Physical injury, even over a short period, is stressful. Sleep deprivation is stressful, as are long periods of hunger and thirst. Being too cold is stressful. Elderly people tend to be more sensitive to the effects of stressors as well as feeling cold more easily, so it is more important for an elderly person than a younger one to keep warm. Frustration of biological needs has become less common in Western society, but it certainly remains an important stressor in many parts of the world.

Psychological need frustration

In modern society it is often the frustration of psychological needs that is the principal cause of stress. Psychological stressors occur when there is a failure to achieve an important psychological need.

American psychologists Edward Deci and Richard Ryan developed a theory called self-determination theory. According to this theory, people have three superordinate (that is, overarching) goals: autonomy, competence, and relatedness.

▶ **Autonomy** refers to the goal of controlling things independently of others.

▶ **Competence** means the goal of being successful, of doing things well.

▶ **Relatedness** means the goal of having good relations with other people.

It is possible to understand frustration in terms of failure to achieve any of these three superordinate goals.

▶ Autonomy and the need for control

There is ample evidence that people have a need for control and autonomy, and to be in charge of their own lives. In 1975 Martin Seligman published a groundbreaking book, *Helplessness: On Depression, Development and Death,* where he coined the term 'learned helplessness'. Seligman and later researchers have shown that, when people or animals learn that they are helpless, this has profound consequences for their biology and psychology. If you find that you are helpless, then not only does this lead to biological changes that promote disease and death, but it also leads to psychological changes. These psychological changes include the experience of depression – feeling depressed – and cognitive and motivational deficits.

A cognitive deficit means that a person's ability to reason or remember is impaired. Helplessness makes people less able to solve complex cognitive problems. A motivational deficit means that a person is less likely to engage in motivated behaviour. Helpless animals will often just sit in their cage and do nothing. Helpless people will often sit on their sofas and do nothing – except watch television.

Learned helplessness occurs when, whatever you do, the outcome remains the same. It is as though you have no ability to influence the world around you. Over time, the inability to control outcomes leads to the person or animal learning that they can never control outcomes – that whatever they do makes no difference at all.

As a general rule, helplessness is associated with negative events, when people are unable to control unpleasant things happening to them. Helplessness is experienced if, whatever you do, your boss is dissatisfied with you, or if, whatever you do, you can't protect yourself.

However, helplessness can also occur when needs are satisfied. It is possible to 'kill with kindness'. Imagine an elderly person in a nursing home where there is no choice of menu, and where, as happens in some cases, the clothes worn by residents are chosen by the nursing staff. All the resident's physical needs are catered for, and the resident doesn't have to make any effort or have any choices at all. Research shows that under such circumstances residents of nursing homes exhibit the deficits of helplessness (depression, motivational deficit and cognitive deficits). However, these deficits can be reversed when residents are required to choose their own food and clothes. Being smothered with kindness is bad for a person.

Sometimes children of wealthy parents are helpless. If they lose their phone, it doesn't matter because 'Daddy' will always buy another one. And if they do badly at school, that doesn't matter either because they will never need to earn money themselves. Learned helplessness occurs whenever a person's actions are unable to affect outcomes, irrespective of whether the outcomes are good or bad.

Helplessness is often encountered in the work environment. If a manager tells a worker what to do, then it is the manager who is in control, not the worker. The more the manager 'micro-manages' what the

The Whitehall Study

The British civil service is a large organization where people are paid at different grades. Some people are paid much more than others. A possible reason for paying more to those at the top would be that senior managers have more responsibility and are therefore more stressed. The Whitehall Study was designed to measure health outcomes in civil servants (the administrative centre of government is based in Whitehall, London). The study recorded the health of 18,000 civil servants over a period of ten years, starting in 1967. The results were striking. Those in the lower grades (such as messengers) had consistently higher mortality and morbidity (diseases) than those in higher grades. There was no evidence that being in a higher managerial position damaged health!

worker does, the more the worker will develop learned helplessness. Helplessness is particular aversive when the worker has responsibilities but no control over the means to deliver those responsibilities.

The Whitehall Study was one of the first to show a relationship between work status and health outcomes. Many other studies have shown that there is a strong correlation between social class and health – the higher the social class, the better the health. One interesting finding from this research is that people in social class one (for example doctors, company directors and university lecturers) have consistently better health outcomes than people in social class two (for example middle managers, teachers and nurses).

The difference in health between social classes one and two is important because these two social classes are very similar in terms of their health-promoting and health-harming behaviours, so the results cannot be explained in terms of the different frequency of health-related behaviours between these classes. Lower social classes generally engage in more health-harming behaviours, such as smoking, as well as having a poorer-quality diet. So the difference in health outcomes between, say, social classes two and three can be explained in terms of these health-harming behaviours.

Because there is minimal difference in health-related behaviour between, for example, doctors and nurses or between lecturers and teachers, there must be something else involved. The consensus is that this 'something else' is stress. People in social class one have less stress because they are more in control of their lives. They do the bossing around rather than having someone else doing the bossing. In addition, those in social class one have more money, and having money helps protect people against the vagaries of life's circumstances. If you have plenty of money, you can control your life much more effectively than if you have little money.

▶ **The need for competence**

We all want to be successful. We all want to be competent at *something*. We don't all want to be successful at the same thing, but we do all want to be competent at *something*. It doesn't matter whether it is at work, at home, at play or at sport. What people normally do is find a criterion on which they can evaluate themselves positively, on which they can show to themselves that they are successful. If Peter is good at sport, Peter will think that being good at sport is good. If Paul is good at music, Paul will think that sport is irrelevant and that what matters is being good at music. So, as a general rule, people do feel successful, and by feeling successful they don't feel stressed. By contrast, failure or lack of success acts as a stressor.

Of course, it is often impossible to rearrange our priorities so that we are good at 'the things that matter'. Some things do matter. Let us suppose that you are a businessman and you lose a contract. It is impossible to pretend that losing the contract doesn't matter.

People can react badly to criticism because criticism is a stressor. Few parents react well to the suggestion that they are failing to bring up their child well. Criticism about choice of clothes, taste in music or food preferences can all cause offence, even where none is intended. Criticism is a denial of a basic human need, the need for competence. Praise, on the other hand, satisfies that basic human need. Flattery often works because it satisfies a basic human need, the need to prove oneself. Flattery can work even when the recipient *knows* it is flattery!

▶ **The need for relatedness**

Humans evolved from primates. Primates are highly social animals. Primates live in groups and groom one another (by picking off parasites from each other). Humans are also social: they were able to survive the harsh rigours of the ice ages only because they helped and supported one another. Humans don't sit around grooming one another. Grooming is effective as a means of social contact only in small groups, and our human ancestors lived in large groups. It has been suggested that speech developed as a way of maintaining social contact when grooming became ineffective due to the increase in group size.

Relatedness is part of our evolutionary history and is hardwired into the very nature of being human. We need friends. We need to feel that we belong. We need to feel that we are valued.

Notice how the top stressor on the Holmes and Rahe list at the beginning of this chapter is that of death of a spouse. Loss of a loved one is highly stressful, not only because it leaves a basic human need unsatisfied but also because it carries the stress of novelty.

Humans lose contact with others not only through death. They also lose friends by being bad tempered, and bad temper can lead to loss of friends and divorce. Later chapters will show that stress makes people bad tempered. However, being bad tempered tends to harm our relationships with others. If a person becomes stressed for one reason or another, their behaviour is likely to change in ways that makes them more exposed to stress. Stress tends to produce a downward spiral, and the effect of stress on social relationships is just one of these downward spirals.

The need for relatedness means that people are particularly sensitive to rejection from others. Criticism has already been mentioned as a stressor because criticism fails to satisfy the need for competence. In addition, criticism can also be interpreted as social rejection – in other words, a double blow.

Because humans have strong feelings of relatedness, watching others suffer can be very stressful. People who have witnessed natural disasters and those who help survivors can be stressed by the experience of watching others suffer. Emergency medical and paramedical teams and the police sometimes report that they experience stress after witnessing others' suffering.

▶ Loneliness

Loneliness is the emotion expressed when a person lacks sufficient social contact. Loneliness is a stressor. Old people who live alone are less likely to be lonely if they keep a pet, and often have better health than those who do not have the companionship of an animal. Animals can act as a substitute for human contact. Indeed, some people prefer the company of animals, although such a preference reveals a poor ability to manage the complexity of human relationships.

With the rise of different forms of virtual reality, there is now evidence of people relating to 'virtual friends', or even 'virtual girlfriends'. Again, such preferences will reduce the stress of loneliness but the choice of a virtual friend or partner provides a sad picture of people who are satisfied with that form of relationship.

▶ Punishment

Whereas frustration occurs when an important goal is not satisfied, punishment occurs when there is a noxious stimulus – typically pain. Pain is a very important stressor. A physical assault on the body produces pain, and pain then produces a stress response. One reason for taking analgesics (painkillers) for acute pain is that pain is a stressor and the adverse effects of pain stress can be reduced by an analgesic. Anaesthetics used during surgical operations are important not only to prevent the patient suffering pain but also to prevent the patient suffering the effects of stress brought about by pain.

In modern society, physical punishment is seldom used for adults – though it was used extensively in the past. Other, subtler but still stressful forms of punishment are now used. For example, imprisonment is a punishment that is stressful, not because it is painful but because it involves frustration. In prison, that important goal, the need to control one's own life, is denied. However, physical punishment (also called corporal punishment) is still sometimes used as a way of disciplining children, even though it has been outlawed in schools in most Western countries.

▶ Child abuse and neglect

A considerable amount of research shows that abuse and neglect are highly stressful for children and have long-term adverse effects. Abuse can be physical (for example, a beating) or emotional (for example, cold and manipulative styles of parenting), or both. Sexual abuse of children is both physical and emotional abuse. Neglect can include emotional neglect and also physical neglect if a child is not fed or provided for properly.

There are cultural differences as to what is perceived to be abuse and what is perceived as 'acceptable parenting'. Sweden was the first country, in 1976, to make it illegal for parents to smack their children and since then the numbers have increased each year. Currently 38 countries ban corporal punishment by parents because it is considered an abusive way of raising children – that is, physical punishment is believed to be a stressor that is harmful to children. However, in many parts of the world, including Asia, the Middle East and the Americas, the smacking of children is considered not only normal but in some cases the right way to bring up children. Views are mixed and strongly held on this matter. Despite its widespread use in the United States, the American Academy of Pediatrics is strongly opposed to physical punishment as a way of disciplining children. Some American hospitals have declared that paediatric wards are 'no smacking zones'. The effects of physical punishment and other forms of parenting on children will be discussed in Chapter 6.

▶ Assault and torture

Physical assault creates not only pain but also a sense of powerlessness, and as a result the victims of physical or sexual violence experience very high levels of stress. The experience of being tortured is extremely stressful because not only is there pain but the pain is associated with uncontrollability, lack of relationship and a feeling of complete subjection.

Short-term stress usually has only short-term effects, but a single episode of trauma can be so stressful that it *does* lead to long-term changes. For example, a single experience of rape can have serious long-term implications for the victim.

▶ Arousal, enjoyment and stress

The alerting response occurs in response to novelty, frustration or punishment. Frustration and punishment are almost invariably experienced as unpleasant, whereas novelty can be negative or positive. Novelty, just like frustration and punishment, increases the arousal of the body (see Chapter 4) but the arousal can be experienced as pleasant.

Fairground rides are exciting. Some are very scary. They create stress responses and yet people choose to go on them. Why is this? The answer comes from thinking carefully about *why* people can experience a sensation that is called *enjoyment*. What is enjoyment for?

One way of thinking about enjoyment is that it is a signal that whatever a person is doing is consistent with their biological make-up. Enjoyment is a signal that *induces people to do more of the same.* People enjoy eating and they enjoy sex. Few people would put substances in their mouths, chew and swallow if it did not feel nice. Nor would people engage in the strange act of sex if it weren't enjoyable. Enjoyment is a signal that has evolved to ensure that people do things that keep them and the human species alive.

Short-term novel events are experienced as positive because humans evolved to manage short-term novel events – as long as there is not too much uncertainty or threat. Our ancestors were hunter-gatherers who, of course, made sure that they did not put themselves in too much danger. The same applies today. No one would go on a fairground ride at the risk of death.

A stressor can cause excitement or fear. It can be interpreted as a positive event or a negative event. Similarly, lack of arousal can be experienced as contentment or boredom. Why should someone be bored rather than content? Why should someone be excited rather than afraid? What makes a stressor enjoyable or aversive? **Reversal theory** suggests that the answer depends on whether a person is focusing their attention on goals or on their behaviour. The stressor always produces high arousal:

❱ If a person focuses their attention on goals (what they are trying to achieve) then high arousal is experienced as fear and anxiety and low arousal as contentment.

❱ If a person focuses on behaviour (what they are doing) then high arousal is experienced as excitement and low arousal as boredom.

Stressors can therefore be enjoyable or not, depending on the focus of attention. Equally, lack of stress is not always experienced as pleasant and doing things you enjoy is no protection against stress!

Summary

There is a wide range of stressors, most (but not all) of which feel 'unpleasant'. Some are short term (acute stressors) and some are long term (chronic stressors). Acute stressors usually have only short-term effects whereas chronic stressors produce long-term change. However, some acute stressors are so stressful that they cause long-term change.

3

Why do some people get more stressed than others?

'The greatest weapon against stress is our ability to choose one thought over another.'

William James, psychologist (1842–1910)

People experience and respond to the same stressor in different ways. There are seven reasons why this happens:

1 People experience events differently due to personality.

2 People value goals differently.

3 People experience different kinds of goal conflict.

4 People cope with stress differently.

5 Social support protects people from stress, and people vary in their level of social support.

6 Exercise protects people from stress, and people vary in their level of exercise.

7 Some people create stress for themselves and others.

▶ Personality

People tend to be consistent in what they do, but they are consistent in different ways. Personality is the study of the consistent differences between people – differences in behaviour that are consistent across situations and time. These consistent differences are described by *dimensions of personality*. A dimension of personality is a continuum along which people differ in terms of their behaviour and their thoughts. There are several dimensions of personality, but the most important dimension, the one that explains most variance, is *neuroticism versus stability*.

The term 'neurotic' has a meaning in common usage, and one that isn't flattering. By contrast, to the psychologist, the dimension of neuroticism – or negative affectivity – is simply a dimension on which people vary and should not imply a value judgement. Nice people can be neurotic!

What is neuroticism? A person high in neuroticism exhibits a much greater physiological response to a stressful event than a person low in neuroticism – low in neuroticism means high in stability. The nature of this physiological response will be described in the next chapter but, for example, the neurotic person shows more sympathetic nervous activity than a stable person when presented with the same stressor. The overall result is that the neurotic person tends to have a more negative mood than the stable person.

About 50 per cent of the variation in personality is due to heredity. So neuroticism and associated mood states such as depression and anxiety are partly due to a person's genes. However, neuroticism is not just a matter of genes: environment plays a role as well.

Research shows that neurotics are sensitive to punishment: they respond more negatively (with more negative mood states) than others when punished. The reason for this sensitivity is, in part, due to a prior history of punishment or negative events. To put it simply, people become neurotic as a result of a stressful life. Trauma and abuse in childhood are known to increase negative affect (neuroticism), but any form of repeated experience of stress will tend towards later neuroticism. Stress breeds stress. The person who has experienced more stress in the past will experience more stress in the future.

The five-factor theory of personality

There are several theories of personality, but the best known is the 'five-factor theory'. According to the five-factor theory, personality varies along five uncorrelated dimensions. The five dimensions are:

1 neuroticism versus stability – the dimension of variation explaining the most variance in behaviour and associated with emotional reactivity and negative mood

2 introversion versus extraversion – a dimension associated with variation in positive mood and the tendency to seek stimulation

3 agreeableness versus disagreeableness – a description of the extent to which a person values positive social relationships

4 openness to new experiences versus closed to new experiences – a dimension associated with willingness to try new things and a dimension associated with spirituality

5 conscientiousness versus non-conscientiousness – a dimension of difference that describes exactly what it says it is.

▶ People value goals differently

People vary in the importance they attach to different goals. The death of a spouse will be highly stressful for someone who is happily married. It will be less stressful, and may be not stressful at all, if a person was planning divorce. A person will not be stressed by losing a bundle of cash if they are comfortably off. But if a person is poor, the loss of that same bundle of cash could be life changing, and thus very stressful.

When considering whether or not a person becomes stressed by an event, the first question to ask is 'To what extent is this person's life changed for the worse?' It is the change in life circumstances that makes a difference. Redundancy is not a stressor for someone who is coming up to retirement. It is a very big stressor for someone who is starting out on their career. For someone coming up to retirement, the redundancy package might be considered a bonus. For someone starting out, the redundancy package is very much less attractive.

Careers may be stressful, not because of any one particular event but because the pattern of life is inconsistent with that person's personality. Round pegs fit better into round holes. A round peg in a square hole is stressful! One of the dimensions of personality (see above) is that of extraversion versus introversion. The extravert is a *stimulus seeker.* The extravert easily becomes bored with repetitive tasks and is most comfortable when there is plenty of stimulation, lots of things going on around them. The introvert will find the same amount of stimulation stressful.

▶ People experience different kinds of goal conflict

Work-life balance is a well-known concept. People's lives should be balanced in terms of their work and their home life. But what exactly does balance mean? The optimum balance between work and home life is not something fixed but rather something that varies between people. A person with few domestic commitments will be happy with a very busy job that involves travel and long periods away from home. A person with many home commitments, perhaps with a young family, will be less happy.

Many people live lives where they have obligations to others and where demands are put on their time. It is not unusual for these many different obligations to be in conflict. Work demands and home-life demands are frequently in conflict.

One might imagine that goal conflict occurs more often in women because it is frequently the case that the woman manages the home as well as having a job. However, it is important to recognize that gender roles have changed over the years, and many men also want to be fully involved with the lives of their children. Coming home late after work and hardly seeing the children can be as upsetting for men as it is for women. Of course, whether or not the stress of work–life goal conflict occurs depends on external circumstances, and this is where a good manager can make all the difference. Recognizing someone's need to go home early on occasion for a school event can greatly reduce stress levels.

Goal conflict occurs in any situation where a person has competing demands on their time, not just those related to work–life balance. A particular example is that of a person looking after a loved relative suffering from dementia. The relative of the dementia sufferer needs and wants to care for the patient. The patient can behave in an erratic way, becoming demanding and even aggressive, but the carer still loves and wants the best for the patient. At the same time, the carer wants to do many other things. The carer wants to enjoy life in the way that life was enjoyed before – but is prevented from doing so due to the burden of care. Research shows that looking after a person with dementia can be highly stressful. Illness creates stress for the ill person but also for those caring for the ill person.

▶ People cope with stress differently

When presented with a stressor, a person makes two kinds of judgement:

▶ What is needed to cope with this situation?

▶ Have I got the resources to cope with this situation?

The first judgement is called *primary appraisal.* At this stage the person has to judge the situation and interpret what it means. The second judgement is called *secondary appraisal.* At this stage, the person works out what to do with the stressor.

Primary appraisal

The interpretation of a stressor varies: it can be interpreted as a threat or it can be interpreted as an opportunity.

What makes one person see a situation as a threat and another as an opportunity? Personality, again, plays a role. People vary along a personality dimension of *optimism versus pessimism.* Optimists are more likely to see the future as benign and a stressful situation as giving rise to an opportunity.

The personality dimension of optimism versus pessimism is closely related to the personality dimension of stability versus neuroticism – though the authors of an optimism scale argue that the two dimensions are distinct. Nevertheless, the strong negative correlation between optimism and neuroticism means that neurotic individuals are not only more likely to perceive a situation as stressful, but they are also less likely to see the possibility of future opportunities if adverse circumstances arise.

Secondary appraisal

Secondary appraisal happens after primary appraisal – after the person has interpreted the meaning of the stressor. At secondary appraisal, the person has to decide how exactly to respond to the stressor.

People vary in the extent to which they believe that they have the resources to deal with new and threatening situations. People high in *hardiness* or *resilience* believe that they have the competence to control the world around them. This perception of competence and control makes them find a threat less stressful than others might. Hardiness and resilience are related to another concept in psychology, that of *self-efficacy*. A person high in self-efficacy believes that they are 'efficacious', that they have the capacity to create change. Notice that self-efficacy can be considered the polar opposite of 'learned helplessness' (see Chapter 2). The efficacious, hardy or resilient person feels in control of the world and can do something about it. The non-hardy, non-resilient, and non-efficacious person feels that nothing can be done and therefore does nothing.

A second way in which people vary in their interpretation and response to a stressor is due to the way they *cope.* The concept of *coping* was introduced into the psychology literature as something independent of personality, in that coping is, at least in part, situation-specific. A person might cope in one way in one situation and in a completely different way in another situation. Subsequently, the concept of *coping style* has been introduced as a way of describing cross-situational consistency in the way people cope with situations. If coping is consistent across situations, then to all intends and purposes it can be treated as a dimension of personality.

There are two ways in which coping theorists have represented coping when treating it as a trait or a dimension of personality. One is to develop broad dimensions, such as *problem- versus emotion-focused coping* or *adaptive versus non-adaptive coping*. Another way is to focus on several individual types of coping rather than aggregate them into broad dimensions. Both ways are described below.

A commonly used broad dimension of difference in coping style is between problem-focused and emotion-focused coping. The problem-focused coper focuses on the problem in hand and how to deal with it. The emotion-focused coper focuses on the emotion experienced in the stressful situation and how to deal with the unpleasant emotion the stressor produces.

Emotion-focused coping can help reduce stress in the short term. By dealing with emotions, the person feels less upset by the stressor. The disadvantage of emotion-focused coping is that it is less effective in the long term.

The emotion-focused coper may become less upset before exams, but the problem-focused coper will do better in terms of results. The emotion-focused coper avoids the situation whereas the problem-focused coper engages with the situation.

Instead of focusing on the broad dimensions of coping, it is also possible to examine individual types of coping. The COPE Inventory (http://www.psy.miami.edu/faculty/ccarver/sclCOPEF.html) is a coping scale commonly used by psychologists, which measures several different types of coping. The authors of this scale do not aggregate the different coping types into, for example, emotion-focused or problem-focused or into adaptive and non-adaptive. They suggest that each type of coping should be interpreted in its own right. The different types of coping are listed below:

Positive reinterpretation and growth	Behavioural disengagement
Mental disengagement	Restraint
Focus on and venting of emotions	Use of emotional social support
Use of instrumental social support	Substance use
Active coping	Acceptance
Denial	Suppression of competing activities
Religious coping	Planning
Humour	

Whether or not coping is treated as a broad dimension of coping style or as several different types of coping, the way a person copes with a stressor influences to what extent the stressor is perceived as stressful. Several coping techniques reduce stress. For example, religious coping enables people to see an unpleasant event as 'part of God's plan' and therefore ultimately benign. Similarly, substance use can dull the senses and make the stressor appear less stressful. However, some stress-reducing techniques – such as denial or humour or substance use – help in the short term but have the potential for greater stress in the long term.

▶ Social support protects people from stress

Research shows that people who experience high levels of social support are less likely to perceive an event as stressful. In addition, if a situation is perceived as stressful, then people high in social support show fewer adverse effects to the stressor. In short, social support *protects* against stress.

What exactly is social support? Measures of social support distinguish between the practical support and the emotional support that others give. A person has practical support if others can be relied on to do practical things. At home, such practical things might include shopping and help with childcare. At work, practical social support is experienced if a member of a team feels that others can be relied on to help with group tasks.

Emotional social support is provided by others who listen to a person and give positive feedback, so the stressed person feels that others understand and are sympathetic to that person's problems.

Practical support and emotional support are both important for reducing stress. Employers can do little to help people develop social support at home, but they can help their employees experience both practical and emotional social support at work. Good managers take care to ensure that people work in cohesive and mutually supportive teams. Arranging an awayday can be one way of helping good social relations at work. Although awaydays are often justified by focusing on the practical, they can also have an emotional benefit in that workers see one another as people, not merely as fellow workers.

▶ Exercise protects against stress

Exercise is a lifestyle choice. People may choose to go to the gym or they exercise without going to the gym – by gardening or walking. The immediate effect of exercise is that it creates the biological changes associated with stress. But if exercise is practised regularly, then those biological changes are associated with less stress. Acute exercise is therefore a stressor, but chronic exercise is (in general) a de-stressor.

Regular exercise has a number of beneficial effects. First, the body adapts to regular exercise so that it becomes less stressed when exercise is taken. A person who takes regular exercise shows a lower increase in heart rate for a given amount of exercise, and a noticeably more rapid decline in heart rate when exercise has stopped. However, regular exercise also creates changes that reduce the impact of psychological stress. Exercise is an excellent protector against stress. There is one exception to this rule. Excessive exercise (such as marathon running) is so stressful that the body does not adapt and so it lacks the health benefits of moderate exercise.

▶ How some people create stress for themselves and others

People do not just respond to their environments, they also change their environments. Some of that change involves the impact one person has on another. In the late 1950s, two American cardiologists, Friedman and Rosenman, proposed a personality type that was predisposed to heart disease, and they called it 'the Type A personality.' The Type A personality is someone who is high in hostility, competitiveness and time urgency. Although the link between Type A and heart disease was researched for many years, the evidence now shows that Type A is part of a more general *disease-prone personality* that contributes to many diseases and not just heart disease. In particular, people with a Type A personality tend to show a greater physiological response to a stressor, as do people high in neuroticism.

The Type A concept is important because a hostile, time-urgent and competitive person is likely to create stress for themselves and for others. Hostility creates a response in others that makes social interactions difficult. In later chapters, it will be shown how hostility, irritability and other negative social emotions are created by stress. So stress produces the kind of social interaction that increases stress. The increased stress then produces the type of social interaction that increases stress. Stress easily becomes a vicious cycle where it feeds on itself.

Summary

This chapter has described the different ways in which different people can respond to the same stressor. People may experience different levels of physiological response to the same stressor and they cope with that stressor in different ways. Stress breeds stress: stress makes people more sensitive to stress and leads to people creating stress for themselves and others.

ALL THAT MATTERS: STRESS

The acute stress response to short-term stressors

'Keep your eyes open, Fireheart. Keep your ears pricked. Keep looking behind you. Because one day I'll find you, and then you'll be crowfood.'

Erin Hunter, Forest of Secrets *(2003)*

The human body is able to make an exquisitely co-ordinated response to any situation that arises. That co-ordinated response helps the body adapt to that situation. The body adapts to *any* situation, not just stressors. When you sit down to eat a meal, your body produces insulin even before you take your first mouthful. Your body is adjusting to the sugar your body expects you are going to eat. Notice that the body doesn't just react to events *after* they happen – the body can anticipate events and adjust itself in advance.

The body's response involves four communication systems:

1 **The behavioural system**, which comprises the brain, the motor and sensory nerves, as well as muscles, bones and tendons

2 **The autonomic nervous system**, comprising the brain and the sympathetic and parasympathetic nerves.

3 **The endocrine system**, which comprises hormones (biochemicals) that are distributed via the blood

4 **The immune system**, which comprises a variety of cells and biochemicals, also distributed via the blood.

Each of these communication systems interacts with all the other three, so it is more realistic to think of the body as having one, integrative communication system. Nevertheless, it is easier to understand this integrative system by examining each of the parts in turn.

▶ The behavioural system

A stressor is a novel, frustrating or punishing event. When a short-term stressor occurs, a person reacts with an alerting response. The person becomes more sensitive to stimuli and is more reactive to stimuli. Part of the brain becomes more active: the part that processes incoming stimuli. The increased activity, the increased awareness of stimuli, can be pleasant. Drugs such as caffeine (and some recreational drugs) have a similar effect in producing pleasant arousal. It is important to note that acute stress, so long as it is not too stressful, can be experienced as positive (see comment on reversal theory at the end of Chapter 2).

Not all parts of the brain become active as a result of acute stressors. Several studies show that, when people are stressed, there is a decline in cognitive ability. In simple terms, people become less able to solve problems when they are stressed. These two different trends, the increase in perceptual awareness and the decrease in cognitive ability, can be understood from an evolutionary perspective. When people become stressed, they tend to revert to primitive, more automatic ways of thinking at the expense of the more complex, cognitive tasks that are required for problem solving. The primitive parts of the brain become more active. The more advanced parts of the brain, those that evolved later in human evolutionary history, become less active.

Although the adverse effect of stress on cognition is well established, very low levels of arousal can also

In one research study, farmers were given a battery of cognitive tests before the harvest and after the harvest. Farmers are poorer before the harvest, and they worry about getting the harvest done and how successful they will be. Farmers are less stressed after the harvest. The results showed that cognitive ability was higher after the harvest compared to before the harvest.

compromise performance. If people are half asleep, they do not perform well. The relationship between arousal and performance is commonly described by the 'inverted U-shaped curve'.

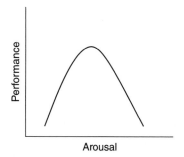

▲ The inverted U-shaped curve

When people are very unaroused – when they are half asleep – performance is poor. As they wake up, their performance improves. However, when they are very aroused – that is, when they are stressed – performance drops off. As a general rule, the more *complex* the task, the *lower* the level of arousal that is needed to cause a decrease in performance. Complex tasks are therefore particularly sensitive to the adverse effects of stress. Complex tasks include tasks involving creativity and high levels of problem solving.

Stress, or over-arousal, is important for memory. When people are highly aroused, their ability to remember becomes much worse. Several real-life examples illustrate this problem. For example, if a student facing an exam is very worried and tries to revise, their level of anxiety and arousal may be so great that their ability to memorize is compromised. The student tries hard and nothing happens. The situation is made worse if the student drinks a lot of strong coffee, as coffee is a stimulant and adds to their arousal.

A second example of how over-arousal can harm memory occurs when patients visit a doctor. Patients can be very stressed when visiting a doctor, either because of their symptoms or because the visit itself can be intimidating. Research shows that patients will often understand what is said in a consultation but then completely forget it afterwards, and may even deny being told something that they were in fact told. Good health communicators are aware of this problem, and they will give patients only a little information to begin with, and will repeat the information to help with memorization.

Stressors influence the way people make risky decisions. Risky decisions are decisions where the outcome is uncertain. For example, a market trader is making a

Communicating in a stressful situation

When patients attend a medical consultation, they will often be given several pieces of information. Of these, they will remember the diagnosis best of all, followed by the prognosis, but they will often completely forget the self-care instructions they have been given. Doctors have found that a good way of communicating with a patient is to use the following sequence: give the diagnosis, tell the patient what to do, tell the patient what to expect, and then go back and tell the patient what to do again.

risky decision when buying some shares because it is uncertain whether the shares will go up or down. The way stressors affect risk taking depends on the nature of the risk. If the risk involves some kind of gain, people are less likely to make a risky choice. For example, imagine a quiz game in which correct answers lead to a doubling of the prize money, but incorrect answers lead to losing it all. A person who is stressed when playing that game will stick with what they have won and not try to increase their takings.

By contrast, if the risk involves loss, then people take more risky decisions when they become stressed. Let us suppose that a gambler has lost a lot of money and is becoming stressed as a result. The gambler, because of the increased stress, is likely to take even greater risks and increase the size of bets – with the probability of losing even more money.

Another example of the effect of stress on risk when loss is possible concerns choice of medical treatment. Let us suppose someone has a disease where there are two treatment options – watchful waiting (where the patient just monitors symptoms to see whether they deteriorate) and surgery. Given a choice between 'watchful waiting' and a new and possibly dangerous surgical treatment that just might effect a cure, the more stressed person will choose the surgical procedure.

▶ The autonomic nervous system

The behavioural system is centred on the brain. Nerves come out of the brain via the brainstem. These nerves can be divided into two groups:

▶ those that support the behavioural system and involve sensation (sensory input nerves) and voluntary control of muscles (motor control nerves)

▶ those that support the autonomic nervous system.

The autonomic nervous system is a system that allows the brain to control the various bodily organs 'automatically' – that is, the body is controlled without conscious awareness. The autonomic nervous system controls things like heart rate, the rate of peristalsis in the gut (the rate at which food is massaged down the gut), respiration rate, and the dilation or constriction of blood vessels.

The autonomic nervous system consists of two branches, the sympathetic and the parasympathetic. The sympathetic and parasympathetic nerves start from the brain and then spread out through the body. The sympathetic nerves activate responses associated with 'fight or flight'. The parasympathetic nerves activate relaxation responses associated with activities that do not require physical effort – such as resting and eating.

The sympathetic and parasympathetic nerves act in opposition to each other: when one system is active, the other is not. When the sympathetic nervous system is activated (by the brain) then the parasympathetic system is quiet, and vice versa. The sympathetic nervous system tends to produce faster responses than the parasympathetic – getting stressed happens faster than getting relaxed.

Stress and sex

Although the sympathetic and parasympathetic nervous systems act as a kind of seesaw, with one going up and the other going down, this is not always the case. In sexual activity, both sympathetic and parasympathetic nervous systems are active. Sexual arousal *is* arousal. The heart beats faster. However, if the person is stressed to the extent that the parasympathetic nervous system fails to become active as well, sexual problems can result. Impotence in males (inability to achieve or maintain an erection during sexual intercourse) is often caused by anxiety and stress about sexual performance. The sympathetic nervous system of the impotent male becomes aroused, but because stress is inhibiting the parasympathetic system, an erection is not maintained. For happy sexual relations, *both* males and females need to be aroused and relaxed at the same time!

When the brain detects an external threat, the autonomic nervous system changes many different parts of the body so that it is adapted to fight or flight. The change is brought about by the sympathetic and parasympathetic nerves that come out of the brainstem. When the sympathetic nerves reach their targets, they release a chemical at the nerve endings, a chemical or transmitter substance called noradrenalin (epinephrine in US terminology). Noradrenalin (epinephrine) causes an increase in heart rate, a more rapid rate of breathing, and many other changes such as reduced blood flow to the gut and increased blood flow to the muscles.

The autonomic nervous system is the 'hardwired' stress alerting system, in contrast to the endocrine system where the alert is achieved through hormones that are distributed through the blood.

The autonomic nervous system is more than an alerting system. It is also a relaxing system, through the effect of the parasympathetic branch. The parasympathetic nerves are responsible for the relaxation response (see Chapter 9). One of these parasympathetic nerves, the vagus, is important for communicating when a threat (acute stressor) has gone. The autonomic system helps the body prepare itself for whatever action is needed.

Notice that the body specializes itself for particular functions. When the external environment is not threatening, then the body specializes itself for *body maintenance*. Body maintenance involves repair to tissues and digestion. When the external environment is threatening, then the body specializes itself for *external threat*, a threat that requires greater resources to be allocated to the behavioural system. It follows, therefore, that the body is less able to maintain itself when under external threat, and so constant threat leads to a lack of body maintenance.

▶ The endocrine system

The endocrine system alerts the body to potential danger through the hypothalamic-pituitary-adrenal (or HPA) axis. The sequence of events is as follows:

1 The hypothalamus (part of the brain) responds to the stressor and produces corticotropin-releasing hormone (CRH).

2 The CRH stimulates the pituitary gland (at the bottom of the brain) to produce adrenocorticotrophic hormone (ACTH).

3 The ACTH stimulates the adrenal gland to produce two hormones, adrenalin (epinephrine) and cortisol.

Notice that adrenalin (epinephrine) and noradrenalin (norepinephrine) sound similar, and this reflects the fact that they are similarly shaped molecules and share similar functions. The endocrine and the autonomic nervous systems work together.

Adrenalin (epinephrine) and cortisol prepare the body for the stressor but they do it in different ways. Adrenalin, like noradrenalin, alters numerous functions in the body and prepares the body for fight or flight. Whereas the action of adrenalin is relatively fast, the release of cortisol in response to stress leads to much slower *metabolic changes* – changes in the way the body uses energy. These metabolic changes prepare the body for long-term stress – something that can have adverse consequences.

The brain is sensitive to the level of cortisol, and if the cortisol level increases it will produce less CRH in response. The result is that the level of cortisol is controlled by a negative feedback process and does not spiral out of control. However, this controlling effect of cortisol on corticotropin-releasing hormone is reduced after prolonged stress, leading to some abnormal patterns where cortisol levels remain continuously high (or, sometimes, low). The level of cortisol in the blood is a good indicator of the cumulative effect of stress over time.

Levels of adrenalin and levels of cortisol vary over the course of the day – that is, they both exhibit *diurnal variation.* In the morning there is a vast increase in both these hormones, and at night they decline so that, by the time a person wakes up in the morning, they are at their lowest level. Some people are very grouchy in the early morning, and then they become less irritable as the morning progresses. Early-morning irritability can be attributed to hormonal levels. Some people become irritable when adrenalin and cortisol levels are low.

Stress and healing

One of the effects of adrenalin is to inhibit wound healing. Adrenalin levels are at their lowest during the night, so wounds heal most quickly during the night and more slowly during the day. Being stressed (with either acute or chronic stress) is unhelpful for wound healing of any kind. Hence, the use of analgesics following surgery can help reduce pain, thereby reducing stress, which lowers the production of adrenalin that is the result of stress, and so aids recovery.

▶ The immune system

The immune system has two branches, the natural immune system and the learned immune system. The natural immune system is a system that responds to any kind of foreign body. Foreign bodies include bacteria, viruses and parasites. A foreign body stimulates the natural immune system to produce chemicals, including pro-inflammatory cytokines.

Pro-inflammatory cytokines

Pro-inflammatory cytokines belong to a class of chemicals called *inflammatory mediators*. Inflammatory mediators circulate through the bloodstream and carry with them the message that inflammation is needed.

The pro-inflammatory cytokines stimulate white blood cells to attack the foreign body and destroy it. The natural immune system's assault on the foreign body is, normally, only partially successful, and after about three days the learned immune system takes over. The learned immune system is a system that learns to recognize particular types of foreign body. The learned immune system deals with foreign bodies more effectively, but it takes time to recognize and then deal with them. When a person develops a cold, the first thing that happens is that the natural immune system comes into play and attacks the cold virus, and then the cold virus is finally finished off by the learned immune system.

The pro-inflammatory cytokines have several functions, only one of which is to stimulate white blood cells into action. Another function is to increase the level of inflammation at the site of infection. Inflammation is a protective device against infection. Inflammation reduces the action of the bacteria, viruses and parasites. When you have a cold, your nose drips because of the inflammation. The pro-inflammatory cytokines of the natural immune system increase the level of inflammation at the site of infection but, because the pro-inflammatory cytokines are distributed through the blood, they tend to increase inflammation systemically – that is, throughout the body.

Substance P

Tissue damage (that is, a physical assault on the body) leads to that tissue releasing a biochemical called Substance P. Substance P is another inflammatory mediator that increases the level of inflammation but it also has another effect. Substance P also stimulates the pro-inflammatory cytokines. Together, Substance P and the pro-inflammatory cytokines have the effect of increasing inflammation *throughout* the body. The effect of Substance P and the pro-inflammatory cytokines is *systemic*, so it is possible to refer to systemic inflammation, or non-specific inflammation, because the inflammation is not linked to any specific system.

Psychological stress (i.e., information mediated from the brain) produces Substance P, and therefore also increases the levels of pro-inflammatory cytokines. The pro-inflammatory cytokines then increase the activity of some of the white blood cells, in particular a type of white blood cell called a *Natural Killer Cell*. Psychological stressors therefore have the same overall effect on the body as tissue damage – and a very similar effect to that of foreign bodies. Stressors produce systemic inflammation. Notice that tissue damage and psychological stress share a similar biological pathway, both involving Substance P. From an evolutionary point of view, the link between stress and inflammation makes sense. The stresses of our ancestors were often situations of physical danger, where tissue damage (from sabre-toothed tigers and other dangerous animals) could take place. So the stressors lead to the body preparing itself for physical assault and hence the need to protect against bacteria, viruses and parasites.

Allergies

One other fact about the immune system needs to be covered before a description of how the immune system relates to the other three systems. Sometimes the learned immune system gets it wrong: it recognizes and interprets a substance that is *not* dangerous as one that is. Allergy occurs when the body exhibits an over-active immune response to an innocuous substance. For example, allergic asthma is a disease where the airways become inflamed. When a person with allergic asthma comes into contact with an allergen, their body produces a substance (immunoglobulin E, or IgE) designed to protect against parasites. IgE then causes a variety of changes that result in inflammation in the lung. People with allergic asthma vary in terms of what they are allergic to: the most common allergens are inhaled substances such as faeces of house dust mites, animal dander (fine dust coming off animals such as cats and dogs) and various pollens.

▶ Some more interactions

The four systems (behavioural, autonomic, endocrine and immune) are often treated as separate, but in reality they are so interlinked that it also makes sense to think of them as one big adaptive system. This section describes some additional interactions to those described above.

Why do we have mental states? Why do we have consciousness? One reason is that mental states act as signals within a system – signals that alter behaviour. The sections above show how the body prepares itself for external events, including stressors. It is also the case that the behavioural system adapts itself to the internal state of the body.

How the immune system influences behaviour

The pro-inflammatory cytokines have an effect on the brain. They induce feelings of tiredness. When an animal becomes injured or ill, it tends to rest. When humans get influenza, they experience a range of different symptoms, including aching limbs and tiredness. These symptoms are not caused by the virus but by the pro-inflammatory cytokines. The behavioural system is designed to reduce activity when the body's resources need to be mobilized to carry out repairs or to deal with infection.

The immune response and cognitive ability

People sometimes feel that, when they get a cold, their problem-solving skills decline and the research evidence supports this. Research shows that the immune response to infection does in fact lead to a reduction in cognitive ability. *Both* psychological stress *and* the biological stress of infection reduce cognitive ability.

How the endocrine system influences behaviour

Adrenalin and cortisol have psychological effects – people given either adrenalin or cortisol notice that they feel different. Research has shown that the effects of adrenalin depend on how the person interprets them. There is usually a feeling of arousal, but whether this is 'good' (excitement) or 'bad' (anxiety) depends on what the person has been told to expect. The effect of cortisol is known from clinical experience because similar products, oral corticosteroids, are used to treat certain diseases where there are high levels of inflammation. Patients sometimes need to take large doses of oral corticosteroids to counteract inflammation. The effects of oral corticosteroids vary between people, but they include a feeling of increased energy (though there are also reports of depression), increased irritability, difficulty relaxing, sleep disturbance and vivid dreams. All these feelings and experiences are also reported by people who experience long-term stress.

How the endocrine system influences the immune system

Cortisol has the effect of suppressing the action of pro-inflammatory cytokines. Cortisol also has the effect of suppressing the action of anti-inflammatory cytokines, but the general effect is for cortisol to reduce inflammation. Drugs related to cortisol are used to suppress inflammation when people have an inflammatory disease. So, when a person is exposed to a stressor, there is an increase in mechanisms that *increase* inflammation and also an increase in some mechanisms that *decrease* inflammation. The result is that the effects of stress are often complex and can vary between individuals and over time.

Stress and disease symptoms

There are several diseases where inflammation is specific to one particular part of the body – in the lung in the case of asthma, in the gut in the case of inflammatory bowel disease, in the nerves in the case of multiple sclerosis, or in the joints in the case of rheumatoid arthritis. Acute psychological stress produces a short-term increase in systemic inflammation. The systemic inflammation interacts with the specific inflammation, resulting in a short-term worsening of symptoms in many diseases, including asthma, inflammatory bowel disease, multiple sclerosis and rheumatoid arthritis. Stress therefore exacerbates many diseases and makes the symptoms of that disease worse.

In addition to the effect of the immune system on symptoms, symptoms of disease are also exacerbated by stress through the autonomic nervous system. The vagus nerve interacts with organs throughout the body, and lack of vagal activation (that is, lack of relaxation) then alters the functioning of those organs. This altered functioning creates symptoms.

The effect of psychological stress on the immune system has important consequences for disease. The short-term effects of stress act to increase inflammation and symptoms of existing disease. The long-term effects of stress act to cause disease onset (see Chapters 5 and 6).

Summary

The human body is designed for short-term stress. It is designed for mammoth hunts and the need to escape from sabre-toothed tigers. Stress in the short term can be experienced as exciting, and many people engage in short-term stressful activities such as sports or fairground rides. However, people are *not* designed to hunt mammoths all the time: they are not designed for long-term (chronic) stress. Although short-term (acute) stress can exacerbate existing illness, long-term stress can cause disease onset. The effect of long-term stress will be described in the next chapter.

The long-term stress response to chronic stressors

*'It is an easy thing to triumph
in the summers sun
And in the vintage and to sing
on the waggon loaded with corn
It is an easy thing to talk of
patience to the afflicted'*

William Blake, The Four Zoas (1802)

Acute stress produces changes in the body that revert back to normal once the acute stress has disappeared. By contrast, chronic stress and traumatic acute stress produce long-term changes that either remain fixed or are difficult to change. This chapter provides an account of the long-term changes that occur in the four communication systems of the body:

1 **The behavioural system**

2 **The autonomic nervous system**

3 **The endocrine system**

4 **The immune system.**

▶ The behavioural system

Reinforcement sensitivity theory is a theory that explains how animals (including humans) change after experiencing either a sequences of *rewards* or *punishments.* In simple terms, reward means something nice happening and punishment means something unpleasant. The theory explains the changes that take place following repeated rewards or repeated punishment.

▶ Repeated reward leads to *reward sensitivity.*

▶ Repeated punishment leads to *punishment sensitivity.*

Punishment sensitivity means that an animal becomes sensitized to punishment. In lay terms, this means that the animal behaves as though punishment is always likely or expected. People with punishment sensitivity have experienced stressors over a period of time – or a very severe stress – and behave as though the world is a stressful place. This expectation that the world is a stressful place affects emotions, and emotions influence cognitions and behaviour.

Exposure to chronic stressors leads to three principal emotions: depression, anxiety and fatigue. These three emotions are highly correlated with one another and they are also highly correlated with the personality dimension of neuroticism (see Chapter 3).

Measuring depression, anxiety and fatigue

Questionnaires are available to measure depression, anxiety and fatigue. Some scales have restricted access and require purchase, but the trend now is for researchers to construct and use open-access questionnaires that are available on the Internet. A simple online search will reveal the PHQ-9 (for measuring depression), the GAD-7 (for measuring anxiety) and the Chalder fatigue scale (for measuring fatigue).

Research on the relationship between stress and depression has revealed an effect labelled *kindling*. If a person experiences stress on a number of occasions (or a major trauma), they may not develop depression on those particular occasions. However, they become more susceptible to developing depression following a further stressful episode. This later stressful episode tips them over the edge and causes depression, but that depression occurs because of the kindling effect of the prior depression. The most recent stressful episode may itself be quite minor, but what the person is responding to is not just the minor stressor but the long history of stressors that occurred before.

Research shows that early life stress increases irritability and hostility. Early life stress includes foetal distress caused by adverse circumstances in the womb, such as insufficient nutrition or infection. Children born with very low birth weight due to stress in the womb tend to have higher levels of hostility when adult. Animals reared in suboptimal conditions (either over- or under-stimulation) are more irritable than normal. These changes come about, in part, due to epigenetic changes that take place as a result of stress. Epigenetics refers to the switching on and off of genes due to environmental influences. Long-term stress effects are due in part to epigenetic changes that 'program' the body towards a stressful environment (see Chapter 6).

Stress and personality

Personality results from an interaction between genes and environment, with each contributing about 50 per cent of the variance. Although there is undoubtedly a genetic tendency for people to vary in neuroticism and punishment sensitivity, this aspect of personality is also the result of the accumulation of stresses that a person experiences from before birth onwards. Equally, happy people (high in extraversion, openness and agreeableness) will have a prior history of rewards, and are therefore reward sensitive. Reward-sensitive people expect the world to be a rewarding place!

Chronic stress alters people so that they become 'the stressed person'. The stressed person is irritable, anxious, depressed and often fatigued, and can on occasion be hostile. A common mistake is to attribute these personality characteristics to some 'bad' stable feature of the person, when they are often the response to a particular sort of environment – a stressed environment.

The psychological changes that take place as a result of chronic stress alter behaviour. Increased levels of stress can lead to an increase in health-harming behaviours. Stress can lead to an increase or resumption in smoking, and stress is associated with overeating and drinking. Stress has this effect because it acts as a 'dis-inhibiter'. People are often aware of the health-harming effects of certain behaviours and therefore try to avoid that behaviour. A person who is trying to diet will be aware that overeating is not good. People on a diet are 'restrained eaters' in that they are trying to maintain a diet through cognitive control. Cognitive control, including cognitive control over eating, is reduced when people are stressed. The lack of cognitive control (the technical term is *ego depletion*) means that the person engages in behaviours they would otherwise avoid. When a person becomes stressed, their self-control starts to evaporate. They binge-eat and do things that they would otherwise find unacceptable.

Chronic stress produces irritability and hostility. If a person becomes irritable because of stress, that irritable behaviour will then alter the behaviour of others, so that they become hostile in return. The stressed, hostile person loses friends and becomes socially isolated. The stressed, hostile person therefore loses the social support that was otherwise protecting them against stress. The chronically stressed person tends to produce an environment that becomes even more stressful. Stress produces a vicious cycle all of its own.

Stressed people are neither good employees nor good employers. Stressed employers make life unpleasant and create stress for employees, and stressed employees do not work well. The obvious solution is to try to control stress at work, but this is far easier said than done because many jobs include external demands that are intrinsically stressful. To be successful, it may be necessary to work in a stressful environment. The problem of work stress is therefore not just a matter of individuals but also a matter of how society is organized (see Chapter 8).

▶ The autonomic nervous system

The autonomic nervous system controls many of the automatic functions in the body. Chronic stress alters the functioning of the autonomic nervous system, and in particular it increases sympathetic activity and decreases parasympathetic activity (see Chapter 4 for details of these two branches of the autonomic nervous system). The autonomic nervous system becomes fixed by chronic stress into a state characteristic of acute stress. That is, the autonomic nervous system is responding as though stress is always present – even when, objectively, the person is not stressed.

The constant increased sympathetic and decreased parasympathetic activity produced by chronic stress alters the functioning of numerous organs within the body. One such alteration is an increase in heart rate. The increase in heart rate then leads to high blood pressure. Other signs of autonomic disturbance include problems with temperature regulation and dizziness. Yet other changes take place in the gut. The gut can become less motile (there is less peristalsis, or movement) under acute stress and this altered gut function can lead to a range of gut-related symptoms, including, but not exclusively, constipation. The autonomic nervous system has far-reaching effects throughout the body. The changes wrought by long-term stress lead to dysregulation throughout the body.

Chronic stress not only alters heart rate, but it also alters *heart rate variability.* The normal heartbeat sounds regular but careful measurement shows that the interval between beats varies slightly. This variation in the interval between beats is a sign of good health – that is, of lack of stress. The reason is that the heart rate is determined by several different factors. High heart-rate variability is an indication that the heart is sensitive to these different factors. When the heart rate becomes more regular, this shows that the autonomic control is less sensitive, and therefore less effective. In brief, chronic stress produces chronic changes to the autonomic nervous system that then produce a variety of symptoms associated with poor autonomic control.

▶ The endocrine system

Cortisol levels vary throughout the day. Chronic stress alters that variation in a complex way, by altering the feedback systems that control cortisol levels. That alteration can take several forms. In the case of moderate chronic stress, there is an increase in cortisol levels. A raised cortisol profile is a marker for increased levels of stress and is the most commonly observed outcome for chronic stress. However, with the most severe chronic stress, there is a reduced level of cortisol. Additionally, in these severe chronic stress cases there is a *blunted adrenalin response* to stressors. The blunted adrenalin response means that the level of adrenalin produced in response to a stressor is reduced. The result is that the highly stressed person actually produces fewer stress-related hormones than the unstressed person. The reduction in cortisol and adrenalin levels is more often found in those individuals with a stress-related illness, a topic covered in the next chapter.

Measuring cortisol

When research on the relationship between cortisol and stress was first investigated, it was possible only to measure cortisol through a sample of blood. Taking a sample of blood is itself stressful. Improved measuring techniques mean that it is now possible to assess cortisol in urine and in saliva. Being able to measure cortisol more regularly and without an invasive procedure is invaluable if diurnal variation of cortisol is being assessed.

The dysregulation of cortisol levels can be explained, in part, by the fact that the normal feedback loop that controls the level of cortisol (see Chapter 1) stops functioning after prolonged periods of stress. Although this book has focused on cortisol and adrenalin, the endocrine system involves many other hormones that are altered by chronic stress.

▶ The immune system

Acute stress produces an increase in pro-inflammatory cytokines and an increase in white blood cell activity. Chronic stress leads to chronically increased levels of pro-inflammatory cytokines but chronically *reduced* activity in many types of white blood cell.

In the case of chronic stress, the body is sending out a message that there is risk of infection, but at the same time the white blood cells are less able to deal with that infection, should it occur. So, rather than thinking of the immune system as being more or less active as the result of stress, it is better to describe the immune system as becoming *dysregulated* by stress. Chronic stress dysregulates the immune system so that it functions less effectively. This dysregulation is the result of environmentally induced epigenetic changes. Chronic stress switches on those genes that produce pro-inflammatory cytokines, leading to a constant increased level of those cytokines (see Chapter 6).

▶ Some additional interactions

Psychoneuroimmunology is the study of how the brain/ mind interacts with the immune system. Early research in psychoneuroimmunology focused on the way white blood cell activity declined in response to psychological stress. Reduced Natural Killer Cell activity was thought important to the development of cancer. More recently, research has focused on the pro-inflammatory effects of stress on the immune system, because many diseases, including cancer and heart disease, have an inflammatory component in their aetiology. The behavioural, autonomic, endocrine and immune systems are not actually separate systems operating independently of one another. The multiple connections between all these systems suggest that they form one big, interacting, system that is distributed throughout the body.

Cortisol has an inhibiting effect on the immune system. Cortisol inhibits the action of *both* pro-inflammatory and anti-inflammatory cytokines, but the net result is to decrease the level of inflammation. In moderate chronic stress, cortisol levels are raised, and this will tend to have a slight dampening effect on the pro-inflammatory cytokines that are increased by that moderate stress. However, in more severe levels of chronic stress, cortisol levels are reduced and this reduction will contribute to an even greater increase in systemic inflammation.

The gut and the immune system

At school, children are often taught that the purpose of the gut is to digest food. While this is true, the gut also has other important functions. The gut is an important organ in which immune learning takes place. The immune system in the gut influences the gut microflora – the bacteria and viruses living in the gut – and these gut microflora then also affect the gut and the permeability of the gut. Nerves from the gut travel to and fro between the emotional centre of the brain (the part called the limbic system). The health of the gut is important for the whole body!

Several diseases involve high levels of inflammation that cause the body's immune system to attack its own tissues. Many medicines are based on modifications of the cortisol molecule and have a similar action to cortisol in suppressing a wide range of immune parameters. These cortisol-related drugs are therefore used to treat inflammatory disease. Recently, a new class of drug, called a monoclonal antibody, has been developed that targets specific inflammatory pathways and therefore has a more specific type of action than the older class based on cortisol – and therefore has fewer side effects.

The immune theory of depression was proposed some 30 years ago. According to this theory, depression is the result of raised systemic inflammatory mediators – such as the pro-inflammatory cytokines. There is some truth to the theory in that inflammatory mediators are often raised in cases of depression, but it clearly isn't the whole story. Treatments that inhibit the action of pro-inflammatory cytokines, including the new monoclonal antibodies, do not cure depression. Nevertheless the co-occurrence of depression with pro-inflammatory cytokines shows that cytokines are involved in some way.

Depression and serotonin

Most psychology and medical textbooks teach students that depression is the result of low levels of serotonin in the brain. While this view supports a billion-pound pharmaceutical industry, the evidence suggests a far more complex relationship. Antidepressants raise levels of serotonin in the brain, and are effective in treating depression. However, research shows that at least 80 per cent of the effectiveness of antidepressants is due to the placebo effect. Less than 20 per cent is due to the active effect of the drug. If depression really were just a matter of low levels of serotonin, it wouldn't be the problem it remains today.

Mood is closely related to the state of the immune system. Mental stress increases systemic inflammatory mediators (such as the pro-inflammatory cytokines), and high levels of those mediators are associated with mood states (such as fatigue) that enhance the natural response to illness. Infection has the effect of increasing systemic inflammatory mediators. The natural response to illness, a response caused by these mediators, is to rest and do very little. Rest following short-term illness is adaptive, but long-term rest can lead to significant later problems because of a gradual deterioration in physiological health resulting from inactivity.

Finally, although this chapter has focused on the four systems, the behavioural, autonomic, endocrine and immune systems, chronic stress produces additional forms of changes. The effect of stress on gene expression – on epigenetics – has been referred to already. However, stress also has an additional effect on cell division. Telomeres are structures involved in the process of cell division and which become shorter and shorter as people age. As telomeres become shorter, the possibility of fatal-disease-related cell mutation increases. Telomeres are part of the body's ageing system. Stress in early life has been shown to decrease the length of telomeres. Stress would appear to increase the biological age of a person.

Summary

Chronic stress produces numerous changes throughout the body, changes that predispose towards disease and inhibit recovery. At the same time, the changes brought about by chronic stress also produce psychological changes that alter behaviour. Not only does stress cause disease through a biological route, but there is also a clear link between the underlying physiology of chronic stress and an increased propensity for health-harming behaviours, such as lack of exercise, overeating, high alcohol intake, recreational drug use and smoking. Chronic stress and acute short-term stress produce *systemic* changes. Depression, fatigue and anxiety are all associated with raised levels of pro-inflammatory cytokines, and endocrine and autonomic dysregulation.

Stress and illness

'It's not stress that kills us,
it is our reaction to it.'

Hans Selye, stress researcher (1907–82)

The simple message is that chronic stress makes illness more likely. To explore this simple message, it is necessary to understand the meaning of illness and its relationship to disease.

Lay people use the word 'illness' to describe a particular kind of experience, the experience of being ill. Being ill involves symptoms of varying kinds – pain, difficulty breathing, constipation, fatigue and so on. People describe themselves as ill when they have symptoms.

The word 'disease' is a technical term meaning that the symptoms experienced by people – or even lack of symptoms – can be explained in terms of a specific and unique *pathophysiology*. Pathophysiology means something wrong with the body. Each disease is defined in terms of its own specific and unique pathophysiology. Lung disease is due to a pathophysiology of the lung (that is, something wrong with the lung), heart disease due to a pathophysiology of the heart, and gastric disease due to pathophysiology of the gastric system, and so on. Different types of lung disease are due to different types of pathophysiology of the lung, different types of heart disease are due to different types of pathophysiology of the heart, and so on. Diseases are defined in terms of a precise classification system of different pathophysiologies.

There are two circumstances when it might not be possible to explain symptoms in terms of a specific and unique pathophysiology, and these two circumstances lead to two other technical concepts: mental illness and functional disorders. Chronic stress is a predictor of disease, mental illness and functional disorders.

▶ Mental illness

The term 'mental illness' is comparatively recent, being used for the first time at the beginning of the twentieth century. During the nineteenth century, symptoms that were behavioural in nature were described as *nervous diseases.* Nervous diseases included hysterical paralysis and depression. The term 'nervous disease' was used because it was assumed that behavioural disturbance was caused by pathophysiology of the brain – that is, nerves. However, despite considerable investigation during the nineteenth century, no specific pathophysiology was found for nervous diseases, apart from one – the disease named after its discoverer, Alzheimer's disease.

The term 'mental illness' began to be used after the Austrian psychotherapist Sigmund Freud suggested a *non-biological* explanation for what were previously called nervous diseases. The term reflected the abandonment of a biological interpretation of disease. The continued use of the term reflects the fact that, despite the discovery of psychoactive drugs, our understanding of the biological basis of mental illness is still incomplete. The term 'mental illness' refers to behavioural symptoms where the biological basis remains controversial. By contrast, Alzheimer's disease is a disease because the underlying pathophysiology is known.

The first psychoactive drugs were developed in the 1950s and their discovery led to hope that there would soon be a simple and effective biological treatment for the different types of mental illness. This hope has not been fulfilled, although psychoactive drugs certainly help. For example, anti-psychotic drugs suppress the symptoms of schizophrenia, but they do not cure schizophrenia. Whereas polio and smallpox have been conquered because their biological basis is fully understood, the biological basis of mental illness is only partially understood – and many people suffer as a result.

▶ Functional disorders

Although the biological basis of many behavioural symptoms remains controversial, it is also the case that no unique and specific pathophysiology has been discovered in some instances of somatic symptoms – including pain, gastric disturbance and fatigue. The term 'functional disorder' is used where there are recognizable types of symptoms that have no discovered unique and specific pathophysiology. Patients are diagnosed with functional disorders by exclusion. If a patient has symptoms that follow a particular identifiable pattern but all biological tests come back negative, the family doctor may diagnose the patient with a functional disorder.

Irritable bowel syndrome is an example of a functional disorder. In the case of irritable bowel syndrome, the bowel looks perfectly normal under the microscope and biochemically. But despite looking normal the bowel behaves in an abnormal fashion – which can include constipation, diarrhoea and pain. Other common functional disorders include fibromyalgia, chronic fatigue syndrome and tension headaches. Less common functional disorders include non-epileptic seizures where a person has an epileptic fit, but the electrical disturbance of the brain that normally accompanies an epileptic fit is absent, and functional blindness where the person's visual system is fully operational but the person remains incapable of seeing.

▶ How does stress cause illness?

The body consists of several organs – the heart, the lungs, the stomach, the gut, the brain and so on. Although these organs are distinct, they do not function independently. They are connected by systems that are distributed throughout the body – that is, the nervous system, the endocrine system and the immune system. The nervous system, endocrine system and immune systems are intimately connected with each other, so they can be thought of as combining into one, integrated, distributed network system. One way of thinking about the separate organs – and their separate diseases – is to imagine them being located within a wider distributed network that connects everything together.

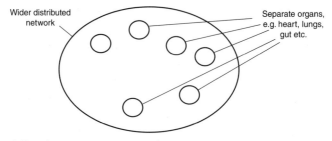

▲ How the organs are connected

The distributed network is altered by chronic stress. This alteration comes about in several ways, one of which is through epigenetic mechanisms.

Genetics and epigenetics

The human genome is a repository of information, information that then influences how the body functions. However, that information is not fixed. Genes can be switched on (that is, they become active) or off (that is, they become inactive) by environmental events. The phenotype differs from the genotype because of these environmental influences that switch genes on and off. Epigenetics, the study of how genes are switched on and off, has shown that stress switches on genes that predispose the body towards chronic inflammation.

Particular genes are switched on or off by the experience of repeated stress or major trauma, and these genes alter how the network operates. Some of the genes switch on the production of inflammatory mediators (see Chapter 5).

The term 'epigenetic programming' is used to describe the way genes become switched on by stress. More generally, one can refer to *body programming* as any form of long-term change, epigenetic or otherwise, that occurs as a result of stress. The most important change from the perspective of disease is the increase in inflammatory mediators. However, the reduction in white blood cell (Natural Killer Cell) activity can also contribute to disease.

Most diseases – that is, most specific pathophysiologies – have an inflammatory component in their underlying mechanism. The increased systemic inflammation (that is, the inflammation in the distributed system) interacts with the specific inflammatory mechanisms so as to increase the specific inflammatory mechanism. The result is that the specific disease is made more likely because of the (non-specific) systemic inflammation. Systemic inflammation increases the risk of most diseases. The reduction in Natural Killer Cell activity also has an effect – it increases the risk of infection and increases the risk of cancer developing because the Natural Killer Cells are particularly effective at removing precancerous cells.

Stress increases the level of systemic inflammation in the body, but many diseases involve inflammation at specific sites (for example, asthma, inflammatory bowel disease and rheumatoid arthritis). The inflammation at these specific sites 'overspills' so as to increase systemic inflammation. The overspill hypothesis demonstrates that, just as systemic inflammation increases specific inflammation, so also the specific inflammation feeds back to increase the systemic inflammation.

The body programming that is the result of chronic stress also makes mental illness and functional disorders more likely, but the underlying mechanism is less certain because the mechanisms of mental illness and functional disorders are less well understood. Suffice it to say that mental illness and functional disorders are associated with a wide range of abnormalities across the nervous system, the endocrine system and the immune system.

▶ Stress through the life cycle

The effect of stress on disease starts from before birth. The growing foetus detects the mother's level of inflammatory mediators, and the inflammatory mediators influence the way the foetus develops. Stress caused by nutritional insufficiency or infection in the womb has been associated with a wide range of diseases in adulthood, including cancer and heart disease. The effect of foetal development on future health is important because there appear to be critical periods when epigenetic changes are more likely to occur. One of those critical periods is during the first trimester of pregnancy.

Childhood is also a crucial time when epigenetic changes can predispose towards adult illness. However, it is important not to lose sight of the fact that stress at any age can produce those epigenetic changes

Stress in the womb

Stress in early life is a particularly important predictor of later disease. James Barker was the first to show that very low birth-weight babies were more likely to develop a range of diseases in later life (hence the 'Barker hypothesis'). Low birth weight is caused by malnutrition or other problems in pregnancy. Biological stress in the womb predisposes to a systemic inflammatory state that increases the risk of all disease. Stress in childhood and later life also predisposes to later life disease, but the risk is particularly great with early life stress.

that predispose towards disease, mental illness and functional disorders. Early life is important because the body is young and plastic and body programming takes place rapidly. Older life is important because disease-causing genes tend to become easily activated with age, so the older person's disease-causing genes are more readily switched on by stress.

The concept of stress in childhood is linked inextricably to child-rearing practices. There are several ways in which parents differ in the way they bring up children but a particularly important one is the use of physical punishment (corporal punishment – see Chapter 2). Research shows that there is correlation between the use of physical punishment and (a) behavioural problems in children and (b) mental and physical illness in later life. However, correlations do not establish cause, and there are two competing explanations for the correlation:

❱ Explanation 1

Physical punishment is stressful and therefore causes the kind of changes described above that lead to illness.

❱ Explanation 2

Physical punishment (in the West, where most research is carried out) is more likely to be used by people from lower socio-economic backgrounds and other factors associated with that background are responsible for the association between corporal punishment and poor health.

There is also a suggestion that naughty children are beaten more often, rather than that it is beating that makes children naughty. The arguments are complex and have implications beyond those of science. These implications include the freedom of parents to do what they like with their own children against society's obligation to protect children from harm (see Chapter 8).

❱ Stress and disease

Disease results from an interaction between a wide range of causal factors. Some of these causal factors are specific to the particular disease. Overexposure to sunlight in people with light-coloured skin predisposes them to skin cancer – but not to heart disease. By contrast, a high cholesterol-producing diet is associated with heart disease. In addition to environmental factors, diseases have specific causes associated with disease-linked genes that are turned on either at random or by particular events. In sum, diseases have many causes *as well* as the biological effects of stress.

Stress affects disease through a non-specific route of raised, systemic inflammatory mediators, and as many diseases have an inflammatory component, stress is a predisposing factor for many diseases. The systemic inflammation combines with the specific disease-causing factors.

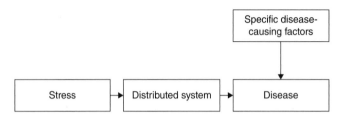

There is some evidence that stress interacts with other predisposing factors. For example, there is good evidence that the risk of asthma is raised in children exposed to dirty air (if they live near a main road or are exposed to second-hand smoke). There is weaker evidence that children suffering trauma are more at risk of developing asthma. However, there is much stronger evidence that children exposed to trauma are more at risk of developing asthma when the trauma is *combined* with exposure to dirty air.

In sum, stress is not the only factor that affects disease onset. Diet, exercise and genetics all play a role. The relative contribution of these different factors is difficult to determine, in part because they interact (see the section at the end of this chapter on stress and obesity).

Not only does stress increase the risk of disease, but it also inhibits recovery. Wound healing is slower in people who experience long-term stress. Caring for a relative with Alzheimer's disease is stressful. People who have looked after a relative with Alzheimer's disease exhibit slow wound healing, long after their loved one has passed away. The reduced rate of wound healing can be explained in part due to the inhibiting effect of stress hormones (adrenalin and cortisol) on healing.

▶ Stress, mental illness and functional disorders

How does stress cause mental illness and functional disorders? A recent theory suggests that the pathophysiology of mental illness and functional disorders has resisted discovery for so long because these disorders are not localized. Instead, the pathophysiology is distributed – in other words, it is an error of the distributed system. The model and its relationship to disease can be represented as follows:

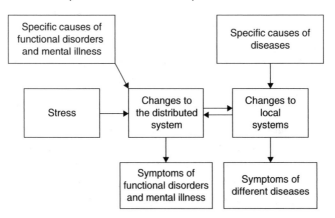

Stress is often implicated in the formation of mental illness and functional disorders. Patients who present with symptoms but are not given a diagnosis are sometimes labelled by their general practitioner or community physician as having 'medically unexplained symptoms'. The term 'medically unexplained symptom' is shorthand for saying that, whatever it is, it isn't a specific disease. Doctors sometimes describe medically undiagnosed symptoms as SLS. SLS stands for 'shit-life-syndrome'. If people have difficult lives, they often present with medically unexplained symptoms. Doctors recognize that a person with a really difficult and stressful life will often present with real and troubling symptoms even when biological test results show no abnormalities.

Stress and mental illness

The relationship between stress and depression was described in Chapter 5, but the relationship between stress and mental illness is far more wide ranging. Evidence shows that mothers who have been exposed to war-related stress during the first trimester of pregnancy give birth to children who, at 15–25 years of age, are more likely to develop schizophrenia. Abuse and neglect in childhood are associated with an increase in all types of mental illness.

Stress does not have to be chronic to produce long-term changes in the body. Extreme trauma can have the same effects. A single event can be so stressful that it produces long-lasting changes. One of the most obvious links between stress and subsequent mental distress occurs in post-traumatic stress disorder, or PTSD. People who have suffered a highly traumatic event, even a single event, will frequently experience disturbing flashbacks of that event. They often feel unsafe, anxious and depressed.

PTSD can occur for a variety of reasons, and not just because a person has experienced trauma. It can also result from watching others experience trauma. The experience of watching others suffer can be deeply stressful, leading to flashbacks and long-term distress.

Stress and functional disorders

Of the wide range of functional disorders, the most common are irritable bowel syndrome (affecting about 10 per cent of those over 50 years old), fibromyalgia (which affects about 2 per cent of the population), and chronic fatigue syndrome, also known as ME/CFS. Rather than consider functional disorders as forming discrete categories, it is now thought that they are best considered spectrum disorders because their symptoms overlap. At least 90 per cent of fibromyalgia patients experience debilitating fatigue – a symptom necessary for the diagnosis of ME/CFS – and at least half of them experience symptoms characteristic of irritable bowel syndrome.

Many patients with functional disorders seek a simple biological solution. For example, they may hope that their problems are caused by a virus which, when discovered, will end their problems. This hope has remained constant despite at least 30 years of negative findings. Scientific

A typical story of ME/CFS

Anne is hard-working student, always near the top of the class. She is a bit of a perfectionist and always does her best. Just before some important exams, she develops glandular fever, and experiences fatigue. (Note: she is tired because of the effect of the pro-inflammatory cytokines produced by her immune system, not because of the virus.) However, Anne is not prepared to let illness get in the way of her success in the exam because her future depends on it. She forces herself to work, and does indeed do well at the exam, despite continuing to feel ill.

Anne gets over the glandular fever, but she remains feeling completely washed out. She finds that she can't do anything, watches a lot of television, and others begin to think that she is lazy – which she finds particularly hurtful because she is desperate to get on with her life, but finds that if she over-exerts herself, she feels much worse the following day. After nine months, Anne is diagnosed with ME/CFS.

logic shows that there must be a biological cause for these disorders. One possible explanation for why it has not been found is that it is a distributed pathophysiology – that it is complex rather than simple. The hypothesis that the cause of functional disorders is due to the distributed system is controversial but the author of this book has taken this approach in his own research.

Stress is implicated in the cause of all functional disorders. In the case of ME/CFS, there is evidence that stress interacts with other factors. For example, infection (of any kind) and injury are also risk factors for

ME/CFS, but the risk is very much increased if infection is coupled with stress. According to the Hyland model, the combination of stress and other factors leads to changes in the distributed system, so that the distributed system is now programmed to produce the symptomatology of the disorder. Treatment requires 'body reprogramming' that is, an undoing of the programming caused by the combination of stress with other factors.

Stress and obesity

Obesity has become a major health problem in Western society. Fat tissue is of two kinds, 'brown' fat that is deposited round the stomach and 'white' fat that is deposited in other parts of the body, for example the hips and bottom. Both types of fat increase systemic inflammation but brown fat in particular has this effect. Hence, fat in the stomach (an apple-shaped rather than a pear-shaped person) is particularly unhealthy. Not surprisingly, obesity (like stress) is associated with an increased incidence of most diseases.

Stress and obesity interact:

▌ First, chronic stressors create changes in the endocrine system that make the deposition of fat, and brown fat in particular, more likely. Stress creates fatness through a biological route.

▌ Second, stress is associated with increased feelings of hunger. Corticosteroids are a drug that mimics the body's own cortisol. A known side effect of oral corticosteroids is that they make people very hungry, sometimes leading to pathological eating behaviour.

Stress creates a preference for high-calorie eating in humans and other animals.

There is another reason why stress leads to greater hunger. Many children are brought up by adults who give them a sweet or candy when they are upset. Sweets or candy have a remarkable effect on unhappy children! However, if a child is repeatedly given a sweet or candy when upset, the child comes to associate sweet food with a reduction in stress. The child grows into an adult who eats for comfort when stressed.

A third reason why stress leads to obesity (see Chapter 5) is that stress is a disinhibitor of restrained eating. Stress makes it less easy to stick to a diet. A stressed person feels hungrier, finds it more difficult to control eating, eats more than they need and puts on weight. The increased weight makes exercise more difficult, so the protective effect of exercise against stress (see Chapter 3) is lost. People may also feel socially isolated because of their obesity – again removing another protective factor against stress. Stress produces a vicious cycle that increases obesity that then increases stress, with an increase in the disease causing pro-inflammatory mediators every step of the way.

It is, of course, true that obesity is the result of overeating, but overeating is itself a symptom of something else being wrong. Obesity is most common not among the most affluent but among the poorest people in Western society. The less well off are more likely to eat non-nutritious fattening food because it is cheap, but they are also more likely to suffer from stress (see Chapters 2 and 3).

Summary

Stress plays a causal role in disease, mental illness and functional disorders. People can try to be healthy by having a healthy diet and taking regular exercise. However, that alone is not going to ensure good health. The level of stress experienced by a person substantially influences their health. As shown in earlier chapters, stress is not always aversive. A person can be happy but still be living a highly stressed life. The advice of psychoneuromimmunologists is: don't stress your immune system. That advice is easier given than followed!

Measuring and detecting stress

'Whatever exists at all exists in some amount. To know it thoroughly involves knowing its quantity as well as its quality.'

René Descartes, philosopher (1595–1650)

It is useful for scientists to be able to measure and detect stress because it helps them to:

▶ understand and manage an individual or group of individuals better

▶ evaluate the quality of stress management

▶ increase knowledge for research or clinical purposes.

This chapter provides an account of several different ways of assessing or detecting stress.

▶ Using direct questions

Even though the meaning of the word 'stress' may not be precise among laypeople when they use it in everyday speech, the general meaning is clear enough. A simple way to measure stress is to ask the question directly: how stressed are you? This simple question can be phrased in several ways, depending on the timescale, for example:

▶ *How stressed are you at the moment?*

▶ *How stressed have you been over the last week?*

▶ *How stressed do you feel most of the time?*

Alteration of the timescale allows assessment of either *state stress* – the stress experienced at a particular time – or *trait stress* – the amount of stress normally experienced.

The question can also be modified to refer to a particular situation, for example:

▶ *How stressed do you feel most of the time at work?*

▶ *How stressed do you feel most of the time when you are at home?*

The phrasing of the question depends on the particular purpose of the stress question – whether to measure the stress of a particular event, for example, or whether to measure the general feeling of stress, and whether to focus specifically on work-related stress or not. It should be noted, however, that responses to these different types of question tend to be correlated. People who experience stress at work are more likely to experience stress at home, because they 'bring home' the stress they experience at work.

The simple, single question of the kinds listed above can provide a useful measure of stress so long as it is accompanied by a scale on which the person can respond. Three formats are commonly used:

1 **A visual analogue scale** where the person marks on a line how stressed they are. For example:

Please put a mark on the line below to show how stressed you feel at the moment.

Not at all   Extremely
stressed_____ stressed

2 **A numeric rating scale** where the person chooses a number. For example:

Please circle the number that best shows how stressed you feel at the moment.

Not at all   Extremely
stressed   0   1   2   3   4   5   6   7   8   9   10   stressed

3 **A category rating scale** where a person indicates a level of stress out of several categories. For example:

Please tick the level of stress you feel at the moment.

Not at all stressed	❏
A little stress	❏
Some stress	❏
Moderate stress	❏
Fairly high stress	❏
High stress	❏
Very high stress	❏

The visual analogue scale is easy to use but has the disadvantage that scoring requires measurement along the line, and (unless presented on a computer) this makes scoring more burdensome. The category rating scale is scored by converting it to a numeric scale (so that, for example, not at all stressed = 0, very high stress = 7), and is preferred by some authors but does take up more space on the page of a questionnaire.

▌ Using indirect questions

Questions about stressors provide an indirect way of assessing stress. Different types of stressor were described in Chapter 3 (such as the extent to which a person feels valued and in control at work). Questions about these experiences can be a useful way of gauging stress in a group of people, but without specifically referring to stress itself.

Useful indirect questions for assessing levels of stress at work include:

- *Do you feel that your line manager values your work?*

- *Do you feel that you can rely on others to help you with your work?*

- *Do you enjoy your work?*

- *Do you feel that you are in control of what you do at work?*

- *Do you experience mood swings?*

Several free-to-use indirect stress questionnaires are available online (see the 100 ideas section at the end of this book).

The measurement of stress levels, either by direct or indirect questions, can help guide the management of individual employees. However, when a group of employees' stress levels are assessed, the results are particularly useful for assessing the competence of managers. Managers have a responsibility to avoid high levels of stress in their workers. Part of this responsibility is altruistic – stress is bad for the workers' health – but there is also a real practical reason for reducing stress. Workers who are highly stressed are unlikely to perform well and are more likely to make errors that lead to accidents.

Self-report methods of stress assessment have advantages and disadvantages. The advantage is that they are easy to complete. The disadvantage is that their meaning is transparent, so that respondents can adjust their response for ulterior aims. Yet another disadvantage is that a person may be happy but stressed – and fail to report it.

▶ Behavioural indicators

Common behavioural indicators of stress are:

▶ a higher-pitched voice

▶ increased peripheral body movement

▶ a change in mood.

The pitch of the human voice is a well-recognized indicator of stress. When people are stressed, their voices become slightly higher in pitch and they also show more variability in pitch. Of course, people vary in their usual pitch, which may be high or low. Therefore it is necessary to know a person's normal pitch before this indicator can be used. However, if a person's normal pitch becomes higher in a particular context, then there is a good chance that the person experiences stress in that context.

People become stressed for a variety of reasons, including when they lie. Stress detection using the pitch of voice as an indicator of lying has been developed commercially for use in mobile phones. However, it is worth bearing in mind that habitual and practised liars are often very skilled at not raising their voice pitch so they are able to hide any 'emotional leakage' that would reveal the lie.

Another behavioural indicator of stress is increased peripheral body movement. Legs and hands move more when people are stressed. Of course, people will try to hide their experience of stress in many social situations, but sometimes their feelings of stress or embarrassment leak out. For example, a person may stand in a social situation with his hands clasped behind his back, but with his fingers constantly moving.

A third behavioural indicator of stress is found in atypical behaviour. Stress affects people in different ways, but a common effect is for a person to become more irritable than usual.

▶ Workplace indicators

Absenteeism

It is normal for workers to become ill now and then and to take time off work. However, some organizations have higher levels of absenteeism than others. Stress is one of several factors that affects absenteeism – for example, absenteeism falls if there are financial consequences. However, if an organization has higher levels of absenteeism than a comparable organization, it is likely that workers in that organization have higher levels of stress.

High levels of stress are the result of poor management. Sometimes the managers of organizations where absenteeism is high respond by punishing the workers who take time off by deducting their pay, but the reality is that it is the managers who are at fault by failing to address the problem of high levels of stress in their workers. High levels of stress will generate more genuine illness and also make workers more inclined to take work off when they become ill. The cause, not the symptom, of absenteeism should be addressed.

High turnover

People who are unhappy at work are likely to leave their job if they have the opportunity to do so. All companies have a level of staff turnover, but if a company has a higher rate of turnover than a comparable company, this is an indication of staff unhappiness. If this unhappiness cannot be attributed to other factors (such as pay or location of work), a likely explanation is that the workers at the company with high turnover are more stressed.

▶ Biological indicators

Assessing autonomic arousal

Short-term autonomic arousal (that is, activation of the sympathetic nervous system) causes increased sweating in the skin. If there is an increased level of sweating, then the conductance of the skin increases (that is, the resistance decreases). This fact is used in the detection of the *galvanic skin response* – a variation in skin conductance.

The galvanic skin response, or GSR, was an early form of lie detector. People become stressed when they lie. When using the GSR to detect lying, the tester attaches electrodes to the skin (usually the hand) of the person being tested. A minute current is passed from one electrode to the other and the tester compares the GSR when a person responds to a neutral question (that is, to a question with no particular significance) to their GSR when they respond to the 'target question'. Although in principle this is a straightforward procedure, in reality, the GSR suffers from many disadvantages as a lie or stress detector. First, the GSR isn't constant but tends to wander slowly up and down randomly. Second, the person being tested knows that they are being assessed and this knowledge allows a potential deceiver to change their behaviour – by generating the experience of stress with the neutral question and trying to be relaxed with the test question.

Long-term autonomic dysregulation can be detected by measuring heart rate variability (see Chapter 5). The heart rate becomes *less* variable in individuals who have been exposed to stressors over a period of time. The disadvantage of this technique is that it requires specialist equipment and software to be able to provide the kind of measurement and analysis needed. Blood pressure is easier to assess and can also act as a measure of stress. Both heart rate variability and blood pressure are measures used primarily in clinical and research contexts.

Assessing the endocrine system

Cortisol can be measured from samples of blood, urine or saliva. Urine and saliva samples are the most readily obtained. However, cortisol levels vary during the course of the day and, although the levels are raised in many people who are stressed, they are actually reduced in some people with severe stress-related illness. Endocrine assessment is used only in a research or clinical context.

Assessing the immune system

Several different pro-inflammatory mediators can be detected in samples of blood. Measurement of immune indicators of stress is useful only in research and clinical contexts.

Summary

For most practical purposes, there are three approaches to stress assessment:

▶ Self-reported stress scales

▶ Behavioural indicators of stress in individuals

▶ Indirect measures of group stress, such as are found in the workplace.

Which one to use depends on the context and purpose of the assessment. Measures of the autonomic nervous system, the endocrine and the immune systems are used only for specialist purposes.

Stress and society

'How beauteous mankind is!
O brave new world,
That has such people in't!'

William Shakespeare, The Tempest *(1610–11)*

So far, this book has focused on stress from an individual perspective. However, individuals live in societies and stress is often linked to societal factors.

▶ Society and biological stress

Chronic stress is an important predictor of poor health (see Chapter 6). Good health is associated with two factors that can be observed at a societal level: body size and longevity. Over the last millennium, human body size and longevity have both increased. People sometimes complain about the stress of modern life, but in reality life is a good deal less stressful than in the past. Of course, the nature of stress has changed over time. In previous centuries, biologically mediated stress (arising from hunger, injury and cold) was more common, whereas now, psychologically mediated stress is more common. Although modern society has been successful at reducing biological stress, it has been less effective at managing new psychological stressors.

Biological stress has not been completely removed in the modern world. Starvation occurs in many countries across the world. The effect of biological stress can be investigated through natural experiments when a population suffers starvation for a short period of time. For example, a short period of starvation occurred after the Second World War in the Netherlands. This has affected the *grandchildren* of those who experienced it, the grandchildren being smaller in stature and poorer in health than normal. The reason is as follows. The human eggs used in reproduction are formed when the female is a foetus in the womb. If a mother is pregnant with a daughter, that daughter's eggs will become programmed by the stress of the mother's experience of famine. The *children* of that daughter then suffer from poor growth and health associated with stress. Stress can skip a generation; a pregnant woman's life programmes the life of her grandchildren.

▶ Society and behaviour control

For a civilized society to exist, it is necessary to have some way of controlling the behaviour of the members of that society. The several ways of controlling behaviour can be divided into two categories: rewards and punishments. In bygone ages, there was a reliance on punishment. People would be whipped for transgressing social rules. They would be put into the stocks or they would be sent to a prison where basic needs were seldom met. Punishments are, by definition, stressful.

Research by behaviourist psychologists as long ago as the 1920s showed that rewards are often far more effective than punishment at controlling behaviour. In recent years, 'cruel and unusual punishments' – those that involve suffering, pain or humiliation – are considered uncivilized and degrading in Western society and people's behaviour is now more often controlled by rewards.

Rewards and punishments both control behaviour, but they lead to different interpretations. When a person's behaviour is being controlled only through punishment, the person interprets the control as loss of freedom. When a person's behaviour is controlled through reward, the person believes that they are free. Imagine that I have asked you to sweep the floor. I can say either 'If you don't sweep the floor I will beat you,' or 'If you sweep the floor I will give you £20.' If I offer you £20, you will happily accept and believe that you are acting out of free choice. If I threaten to beat you, then you will feel you are being forced to act, and you will sweep the floor grudgingly.

Many years ago, the behavioural psychologist B.F. Skinner (1904–90) argued that freedom is an illusion. Behaviour is always controlled. However, when our behaviour is controlled by reward, this provides the illusion of freedom. When behaviour is controlled by punishment, this provides the illusion of servitude.

It seems obvious that punishment is stressful. It is less obvious that rewarded behaviour – behaviour carried out from free will – can also be stressful. Rewarded behaviour is often perceived as non-stressful because it is done out of choice. However, activities performed through choice can be stressful if stressful activities are rewarded. If people are rewarded for working long hours, if overworking is the norm, then people will overwork.

B.F. Skinner's ideas of reward and punishment were incorporated into a novel: *Brave New World* by Aldous Huxley (1932). In his novel, Huxley tells of a society where everyone's behaviour is completely controlled. However, behaviour is controlled entirely by reward; there is never any punishment. The result is that everyone is supremely happy. But there is no freedom; people are not free to do anything except what is decided by the 'controllers', who cleverly manipulate behaviour through the use of reward.

The title of Huxley's book comes from Shakespeare's play *The Tempest*, quoted at the beginning of this chapter. Both the play and the book examine the interplay between a controlled and well-ordered environment versus freedom, and where freedom may create chaos.

▶ Societal goals and stress

Failure to achieve important goals is a stressor (see Chapter 2). Although some of these important goals (such as the need for control, competence and relationships) are universal, there are substantial variations between societies in the way goals are expressed. People's goals are determined to a large extent by the society in which they live.

If, within a particular society, high value is placed on things that most people achieve, then most people will experience few stressors. However, if high value is placed on things that few achieve, then many people will experience stressors.

Stress and goals

If you have just one donkey and you live in a society where the most you can expect is one donkey, then you will be satisfied and unstressed. However, if you have one car and all your friends and neighbours have two cars, then you will feel frustrated. Your lack of an extra car will act as a stressor.

It follows that societies that emphasize material achievement will tend to create situations where people feel dissatisfied with what they have achieved. In 1993, psychologists Tim Kasser and Richard Ryan published a paper entitled 'A dark side of the American dream: correlates of financial success as a life aspiration'. The authors showed that people who put a high value on financial success tended to be less happy than those for whom financial success was less important. Of course, research also shows that *having wealth* is associated with less stress (see Chapter 2). So, being wealthy is good – as long as you aren't motivated to be wealthy! The recommendation I give my students is to marry wealth – they see the logic of the argument and it always gets a laugh.

Overambitious goals create stress and detract from health. Societies vary in the extent to which unattainable goals are encouraged, and they therefore vary in the extent to which people experience stress. When a group of people have a high life expectancy – such as people living in the Japanese island of Okinawa – it is common to examine their diet because of a widespread belief that health is primarily due to diet. The reality is that the diets of people with high life expectancy are very variable. There is one common factor in societies where people have a high life expectancy: people are happy with their lot. People are not trying to achieve what is seldom attainable.

Desire and suffering

One of the famous sayings in Buddhism is that desire is the root of all suffering. Other causes of suffering are hatred and delusion. It follows that if you have vaulting ambition, you will never be satisfied. However, there is an opposite argument that if you have no ambition, you will not achieve even the bare necessities of life.

If parents expect their children to excel at school, then children will often develop the same values as their parents and wish to excel. However, only one person can be top of the class. If everyone wants to be top of the class, then all but that one person will be disappointed.

People work long hours because they are rewarded for working long hours. The European Working Time Directive limits the amount of time that a person should work to 48 hours per week – or, more precisely, it says that working time should not exceed an average of 48 hours in any seven-day period. This directive reflects the fact that overwork is a chronic stressor (see Chapter 5), and the directive goes on to recommend that 'an employer should take all reasonable steps' to ensure that this time limit is maintained with their staff.

Stress can cause erratic behaviour. Although a person remains responsible in law for their behaviour even when stressed, if they break the law their penalty can be reduced if a judge deems that stress was a causative factor.

The reality is that some people work very long hours that are beyond the European directive. Given a choice between overworking and being out of work, many people choose overworking. People perceive that they are free to make that choice when they *choose* activities that create chronic stress. It is unfair to say that such stress is self-inflicted: people cannot isolate themselves from the effects of society. Humans are social beings.

Modern society has become increasingly adept at satisfying the material needs of its members, and it does this by encouraging aspiration and achievement. But that very same aspiration and achievement, which has done so much to make life easier for all of us, has a dark side: it is associated with an increased incidence of stress. The increased incidence of stress is associated with poor health and unhappiness. It can come as no surprise, therefore, that some people decide to 'opt out' of the rat race. And yet such opting out is not really possible, because, ultimately, we are all dependent on one another.

There is a tension between ensuring freedom and protecting the members of a society from themselves. There is a tension between laws that are enacted to protect people from their own desires and the value placed on freedom. Dangerous drugs are made illegal because of the harm done to people who take them, but the laws vary between countries. Equally, laws governing the corporal punishment of children vary between countries. Although the harm caused by stress is recognized by lawgivers, the way they react to that problem varies from country to country. Many societies, however, have laws or codes of practice that require managers, CEOs and board members to be aware of and reduce the impact of stress on their employees – and that duty of care extends to preventing stress from clouding their own judgements.

Summary

Over the course of history, biological stresses have decreased but psychological stresses have not. Improved economic production and wealth have helped people avoid biological stress, but psychologically mediated stress remains a problem. A utopian society is one where both biological and psychological stress are minimized, as suggested in Aldous Huxley's novel *Brave New World*. But whether one wants to live in that 'brave new world' is a matter of debate – it would appear from the end of the novel that Huxley thought not.

Reducing the impact of stress: the relaxation response

'Do not dwell in the past, do not dream of the future, concentrate the mind on the present moment.'

Gautama Buddha, philosopher (sixth century BCE)

It is almost impossible to avoid stress completely. However, it is possible to mitigate the effect of stressors when they do occur, by encouraging the relaxation response. There are four ways of doing this, which are:

▶ relaxation techniques

▶ psychotherapy

▶ complementary and alternative medicine

▶ other activities that have a relaxing effect on the body.

▶ Stress and relaxation

The relaxation response is the opposite of the stress response. The relaxation response reduces autonomic arousal, reduces adrenalin and cortisol, and reduces the inflammatory response. Acute stressors produce a short-term stress response. Short-term relaxation produces a short-term relaxation response. Chronic stressors produce a long-term stress response. Repeated relaxation produces a long-term relaxation response. Chronic stressors lead to epigenetic changes, where genes that increase inflammatory mediators are switched on. It is unclear at the moment to what extent the switched-on inflammatory genes are switched off by long-term relaxation, but the available evidence suggests that chronic relaxation can at least mitigate the effect of chronic stress. The relaxation response can undo at least some of the harm that is caused by chronic stress.

The relaxation response requires *mental* relaxation. Mental relaxation is most often accompanied by physical relaxation (that is, relaxation of muscles), but the two don't necessarily go together. It is possible to be physically relaxed while the mind is racing and worrying about things. There are also some relaxation techniques (such as t'ai chi, yoga and the Alexander technique) where the body is moving, and therefore not entirely relaxed, but it is nonetheless still possible to achieve mental relaxation.

Mental relaxation is important for reducing chronic stress. Chronic stress produces body programming through epigenetic and other mechanisms (see Chapter 5). Chronic stress leads to the body encoding information that the world is a place where primary goals are not met, including safety goals. By contrast, chronic mental relaxation produces *body reprogramming*, where the programming of the body returns to its pre-stress programmed state. This body reprogramming requires the body to encode new information, information that the world is a safe place. The techniques that produce a relaxation response do so by making the body enter a state that the body interprets as safety. It is possible to relax only when feeling safe. Through relaxation, the body learns over time that the world is not dangerous. Notice that relaxation techniques require the person to *experience* relaxation. It is not enough to think or pretend that the world is safe. Body reprogramming is most effective when the body *experiences* the world as a safe place.

▶ Relaxation techniques

Different organizations and people promote relaxation techniques of varying kinds, sometimes with the suggestion that their particular technique is superior to all others. There is no evidence that any one is better than any other but there *is* evidence that, if people do any of these techniques, health-related benefits follow. What is important is not the type of technique, but whether a technique is practised.

Stress has been part of the human experience for millennia. It will come as no surprise, therefore, to learn that techniques for mitigating the effects of stress have also been around for millennia. Historically, these techniques are described by the term 'meditation'. Meditation techniques were developed in both the East and West.

The many different meditation techniques have one thing in common. They stop the normal, seemingly random pattern of thoughts that go through a person's mind. The normal pattern of thoughts is interrupted because the meditator focuses on just one thing. That one thing becomes the focus of the meditation.

Word repetition

The earliest form of meditation developed out of Hindu religious practice in India at least 3,000 years ago. The practice involved *either* the chanting of a single word or phrase out loud, *or* the repetition of that single word or phrase mentally and in silence. The single word often had spiritual significance – for example, the repetition of the word *om*, where *om* symbolizes the divine or absolute reality. A Westernized version of this repetition of a significant word is found in recommendations to repeat the words 'peace' or 'calm'.

The form of meditation based on word repetition is sometimes called *mantra meditation*. In ancient India, mantra meditation was found to have stress-relieving health benefits, and was incorporated into the system of Hindu traditional medicine called Ayurvedic medicine. Meditation is considered the most important therapeutic intervention in Ayurvedic medicine, despite the tendency in the West to focus more on the herbal medicines of the Ayurvedic system. Mantra meditation forms the basis of transcendental meditation, a form of meditation that became popular in the 1960s and 1970s when the Beatles pop group adopted it.

The idea of repetition as a form of relaxation or meditation is not unique to the Hindu tradition. At about the same time that transcendental meditation was being promoted, an American cardiologist, Herbert Benson, published his book *The Relaxation Response*, which provided a non-religious, scientific basis for meditation. Among the many techniques Benson recommended was counting: people are asked to focus on repeating a set of numbers, for example, 1, 2, 3, 4, 5 … 1, 2, 3, 4, 5 … 1, 2, 3, 4, 5.

Word repetition often occurs in rituals and in prayer. There are several examples of repetitious prayer in the Christian tradition, including the Lord's Prayer and the Hail Mary.

The type of technique is unimportant; all relaxation techniques have been shown, when practised over time, to have the biological and psychological consequences of a relaxation response. Preferences vary. Using a preferred technique is a good predictor of effectiveness; in fact, preference is a good predictor of the success of any therapeutic intervention.

Mindfulness

Gautama Buddha was a Hindu prince who, about 2,600 years ago, developed a philosophy now known as Buddhism. Buddhism provides a variety of recommendations for a happy and healthy life, including a form of meditation that in the West is known as *mindfulness*.

In its simplest form, mindfulness involves the person focusing their attention on their breathing. The person focuses on the experience of breathing in and breathing out. As is the case with mantra meditation, mindfulness requires attentional focus. Focused attention on breathing (or 'breath watching') is just one form of mindfulness. Other forms include looking at a candle and focusing on the flame, or focusing on a spot on a wall. Yet other forms of mindfulness involve focusing on the experience of being and the feelings that are being experienced.

The underlying principle of mindfulness is to be mindful of the present. Mindfulness, in its varying forms, involves focusing attention on what is happening at that very moment in time rather thinking about the future or the past. Mindfulness involves being mindful of the present moment in a totally non-judgemental way.

The popularity of transcendental meditation has waned since the 1960s and 1970s, for a variety of possible reasons. More recently, mindfulness has become popular, possibly because it has become distant from its Buddhist origins. The term 'mindfulness' is now used rather than 'mindful meditation'. Perhaps most significantly, mindfulness has been adopted by practitioners of cognitive behaviour therapy. Cognitive behavioural therapy, or CBT, has become the psychotherapy most accepted by the medical community. Mindfulness-based CBT provides a rationale for this particular form of relaxation without the complication of a religious background or concepts from Eastern traditional medicine that are questioned by scientists. Mindfulness-based CBT provides the legitimization of the mindfulness technique through association with a 'legitimate' form of psychotherapy.

Living mindfully

Although it originated in India, Buddhism has had a major influence on philosophy in China and Japan, where its combination with local traditions has created 'Zen Buddhism'. Samurai training derives in part from Zen Buddhism. A friend of mine told me that his Japanese judo teacher was trained, from childhood, as a samurai. As a child, a samurai was taught to walk and not run, so as always to be mindful of his surroundings. By always being mindful of where he was, the samurai could not be taken by surprise. When walking down the street, consider how often you are mindful of your surroundings and how often your thoughts are on other things.

Mindfulness can be incorporated into everyday life. People with gastric problems are sometimes advised to engage in mindful eating, rather than eating while watching television or reading. Mindfulness can be practised in everyday activities, such as doing the washing up or walking. Creative people sometimes talk of 'entering the zone' where they become completely mindful of the practice of their art. Attention is focused on the doing of something, on being in the present of doing, and not on the future goal of achievement.

Positive psychology techniques

The term 'positive psychology' was coined by Martin (Marty) Seligman to provide a contrast with cognitive behavioural therapy (CBT). The aim of CBT is to identify and challenge negative thought patterns, with the goal of eliminating those thought patterns completely. The aim of positive psychology is to encourage positive thought patterns. The rationale is that, once positive thought patterns are established, the negative thought patterns will go away by themselves.

All positive psychology techniques take the form of asking the person to imagine something positive. As is so often the case with any new idea in psychology, related ideas have appeared before. The Velten technique, developed some 50 years ago, requires a person to read out loud a series of positive statements, such as 'I feel cheerful and lively' and 'I'm in a good position to make a success of things today.' The aim of the Velten technique – as with positive psychology – is to raise mood. Going back yet further in time, the use of positive imagery features in both Buddhist practice (focusing on loving another person and then directing that love to oneself) and the medieval Christian tradition, where a knight – or other high-born person – would meditate, for example, on the love of Jesus. Positive imagery creates a sense that the world is safe – and this message to the body then creates the body reprogramming needed to undo the effects of stress.

Several imagination and visualization techniques have been developed under the banner of positive psychology, or at least under its influence. These techniques include gratitude therapy, acceptance and commitment therapy, and self-loving therapy. As with any therapeutic technique, the practice can vary. Gratitude therapy, for example, can take various forms. In one form, the person is asked to write a letter thanking someone for something they did that was kind. In another, the person is asked to think about three things that happened that day that they were grateful for. There is no evidence that any one form of therapy is better than any other – except for the fact that individual preference will vary and it is the preferred technique that usually predicts a better outcome.

Positive psychology techniques involve some form of mindfulness, because the person practises being mindful of the particular positive experience. Much positive psychology can therefore be considered a combination of mindfulness with positive visualization. The mindful state is associated with positivity, with the result that relaxation is associated with positivity – which provides an enhanced message to the body that the world is safe. There is some limited evidence that mindfulness plus positive visualization is more effective than mindfulness alone.

Note that the best predictor of effectiveness of any relaxation technique is whether or not it is actually practised. Techniques for improving adherence to a technique (such as attending a class versus self-help) are therefore also predictors of a better outcome.

▶ Psychotherapy

There are some 200 different kinds of psychotherapy. The different types of psychotherapy can be divided into four main groups:

▶ **Cognitive behavioural therapy**, or CBT, one of the currently most respected (and hence most recommended) forms, helps clients to challenge their negative thoughts. By challenging their negative thoughts, people find that the world seems a less bad or stressful place than it appeared before.

▶ **Psychodynamic approaches** to psychotherapy (including Freudian, Jungian and Adlerian therapists) focus on past stressful events, with the aim of relieving the burden of that prior stressor.

▶ **Existential psychotherapy** focuses on the meaning of a person's life and how that meaning can be achieved in the future – thereby making the future a better place.

▶ **Rogerian counselling**, also known as person-centred therapy, focuses on the relationship between the client and therapist, where a positive environment of unconditional positive regard allows the client to self-heal.

There has been a considerable amount of research on psychotherapy: about 200,000 research papers have been published on the topic. The research shows that psychotherapy is effective. For example, psychotherapy is at least as effective as drug therapy for depression, and probably more effective. However, much remains unknown. The main 'unknown' is *why* psychotherapy is effective. The research evidence shows that all bona fide psychotherapies have almost identical levels of effectiveness. The difference in effectiveness between different psychotherapies accounts for, at most, 1 per cent of the variance in outcome. The similarity in psychotherapy effectiveness is known as 'the Dodo bird effect'. This curious label dates from a paper published in 1936 by Saul Rosenzweig, who quoted from Lewis Carroll's novel *Alice in Wonderland.* When asked who has won a competition, Alice replies, 'Everybody has won and all must have prizes.' The conclusion from Rosenzweig's paper and from numerous research papers since then is that the effectiveness of all psychotherapies is either the same or very nearly the same.

Self-determination theory suggests that humans have a basic and important need for *relatedness.* Lack of relatedness – lack of satisfactory social interactions – creates health problems. The effectiveness of psychotherapy may arise, in part, because it satisfies the need for relatedness. During the psychotherapeutic encounter, the client feels valued, cared for and understood.

The conclusion of the Dodo bird effect (equality of all psychotherapies) does not apply to treatments for post-traumatic stress disorder, or PTSD (see Chapter 6), a disorder where patients experience flashbacks of the traumatic event. Here, there is evidence that some treatments are better than others. One treatment often recommended for PTSD is eye-movement desensitization and reprocessing (EMDR). During EMDR, the client thinks about the traumatic event while the therapist moves an object from right to left, instructing the client to follow the movement with their eyes. The underlying principle is that the coupling of lateral eye movement disrupts the encoding of the trauma. While it is not clear whether EMDR is working because of its purported mechanism, reviews of several studies show that two types of therapy, EMDR and trauma-focused CBT, are more effective in reducing the symptoms of PTSD than non-trauma-focused psychotherapy.

Whether or not psychotherapies are equally effective, it is clear that all *therapists* are not equal. Some therapists are far more effective than others, irrespective of the type of therapy, their age, their gender or length of training. The therapist effect accounts for about 10 per cent of the variance – far more than the variance accounted for by different therapies. The reason for differences in therapist effectiveness is not known, but the relationship between the therapist and client is important. The client's perceived relationship with the therapist predicts outcome.

Whatever the reason for the effectiveness of psychotherapy, the evidence shows that 'talking therapy' does help people overcome the adverse effects of stress. There is also evidence that 'just talking' helps, without the need for formal psychotherapy (see later in this chapter, with reference to support groups). The stress-relieving effects of just talking can be understood in terms of self-determination theory (see Chapter 2), where one of the main human goals is that of relatedness. Talking is a way of achieving that important human goal.

The saying 'A trouble shared is a trouble halved' reflects the belief that just talking about something stressful can reduce that stress. It is worth noting that psychotherapy typically involves talking about troubles. Just talking does help, but why exactly it helps remains controversial. The research evidence from psychotherapy shows that some people are 'good listeners', in that they produce better results when a person talks about their troubles. A good listener does not have to be a psychotherapist. Talking to a 'good listener', irrespective of their prior training, will help reduce the effects of stress.

▶ Complementary and alternative medicine

The term 'complementary and alternative medicine', or CAM, refers to any form of medical treatment that is not usually part of the conventional, state provision of medical care. Two conclusions can be drawn about CAM. First, compared with *no treatment*, all the different CAMs are effective. Second, some of the mechanisms suggested by CAM treatments are not supported by the research evidence.

CAMs may be effective because they provide a caring, supportive social environment. However, several forms of CAM satisfy the fundamental human need for relatedness, and they also provide a process that encourages relaxation by providing cues of safety. Several forms of CAM, in addition to their pro-social effects, have either an explicit or an implicit reference to relaxation.

The Alexander technique

The Alexander technique is not the best-known CAM but it is of particular interest because of its specific reference to relaxation. The technique is named after Frederick Alexander (1869–1955), an actor who found that he was losing his voice during performances. After careful observation of himself in mirrors, he came to the conclusion that his voice loss was due to him adopting a 'stressed posture' when acting. After treating himself, Alexander then went on to treat other actors and, following that, he started treating other people who were reporting stress-related problems.

The Alexander technique works by teaching clients to stand and move in a relaxed way. Sometimes, when people stand or sit, they use muscles that are not needed to keep the body upright. That is, they constantly use muscles that are associated with movements that occur when the body is under stress. Psychological theory independent of the Alexander technique (for example the James–Lange theory) shows that people use cues from the body to interpret their emotions. Thus, if a person uses muscles associated with stress, then the person's body learns that it is under stress.

In the case of Alexander training, the therapist helps the client to relax, using several forms of suggestion to achieve that end. For example, the therapist may suggest that clients imagine a string at the top of their head, which helps them expand their spine upwards. The technique uses suggestion coupled with simple, static or slow-moving exercises to produce relaxation.

Several other techniques following on from the Alexander technique have been developed, including Pilates and several types of exercise to music.

Smiling to reduce stress

Research shows that, if people smile, then they respond less to a stressor than if they were not smiling. The smiling is more effective if it is genuine, but still works even if it is not. In this research study, people were asked to hold a pencil sideways in their mouths – so as to produce an artificial smile. This position reduced the stress response when exposed to a stressor.

Qigong, t'ai chi and yoga

Qigong and t'ai chi both feature as part of traditional Chinese medicine. Technically, t'ai chi is a form of qigong but, in most modern usage, qigong refers to a slightly slower (sometimes static) form of the exercise, whereas t'ai chi is faster – but in both cases the exercise is slow. Yoga features as part of traditional Indian (Ayurvedic) medicine, and most commonly involves very slow or static poses.

In these different techniques of Eastern origin, movement is combined with mental relaxation. When engaging in the slow or static exercise, the client is encouraged to be mindful of the activity itself or to engage in positive visualization of one kind or another. Clients may be encouraged to practise in peaceful and pleasant surroundings, for example in a park or in front of a lake. The different forms of practice create an association between a positive psychological state and relaxation with simple bodily movement. Research evidence shows that, compared with no treatment, these different forms of exercise have a variety of health-promoting benefits.

Massage and touch

Several CAM techniques involve the therapist touching the client. Physical touch can be relaxing (note: humans evolved from primates that groom one another) and massage is a ritualized type of touching. Massage takes various forms, including:

▶ Swedish massage, which involves gentle stroking

▶ reflexology, which involves massage of the feet

▶ the Bowen technique, which involves the very lightest of touches applied to different parts of the body.

The experience of all these techniques is deeply relaxing and clients will sometimes fall asleep. In addition, touch stimulates one of the body's hormones, oxytocin. Oxytocin is the 'feel good' hormone and is associated with positive social interactions (and the let-down response when mothers breastfeed). The research evidence shows massage to be comparable in effectiveness with psychotherapy for treating depression.

Research shows that preterm infants – who experience stress by virtue of their preterm birth – respond well to gentle massage. Massaged preterm infants put on weight faster, leading to earlier discharge from hospital. Additionally, the massaged infants were less likely to have later behavioural problems as children. Research also shows that depressed grandparents experience less depression after massaging their infant grandchildren.

Spiritual healing and reiki

Spiritual healing takes several forms, including reiki. The client lies on a couch (or in a comfortable chair) and the therapist holds their hands about a foot away from the client. The attention of the therapist, the quiet setting and the meaning attached to the situation all create a sense of deep calm. Healing offers a form of intimate social interaction without touch and without talking. The client is provided with a context where it is possible to relax and feel completely safe. One research study showed that 'sham' healing by non-trained healers was as effective as the healing by qualified healers – but they were both effective in that they produced health benefits.

During the nineteenth and the first part of the twentieth century, doctors would sometimes prescribe 'rest' as a treatment for illness. The rest cure, as it was known, was based on the observation that resting could indeed have a healing effect. Making lifestyle changes that involve taking more rest can be helpful in counteracting the effects of stress.

Talking about a problem can help reduce the stressfulness of that problem, due to the protective effect of social support against stress (see Chapter 3). Large organizations often provide support for staff through their human resources departments, including counselling for stressed employees. Smaller organizations can buy that support from independent support organizations.

Illness is a stressor and some people find that joining a support group helps. Support groups exist for most chronic and life-threatening illnesses. In addition to social support, patient support groups provide information, and information reduces uncertainty – uncertainty increases stress (see Chapter 2).

Moderate exercise protects against stress. Exercise does not have to involve high levels of exertion to be healthy. As shown by qigong, t'ai chi and yoga, the level of exertion can be slight. Walking is a healthy and relaxing activity; there is some evidence that walking in the countryside (the 'green gym') or near the seaside (the 'blue gym') confers particular health benefits. The implication of the green gym and blue gym research is that exercise has particular benefits for health and is more relaxing if it is carried out in an environment that is perceived to be pleasant.

Going to a spa is a pleasant activity that combines relaxation with gentle exercise, for example gentle swimming. However, it is not necessary to go to an expensive spa to experience the relaxation that spa treatment can achieve. Many people find a warm soak in the bath to be relaxing and a useful antidote to a stressful day. When having a warm soak, some people modify the bathroom environment with candles, so as to produce a welcoming and even more relaxing atmosphere.

Environments are important to relaxation and to health. In one study, people whose hospital rooms overlooked green fields had a faster rate of recovery than those whose rooms overlooked a car park. Other studies have confirmed that people experience less distress from clinical procedures when exposed to pleasant sensory stimulation – pictures and sounds of the natural world and potted plants in waiting rooms. Studies have also confirmed the health-promoting benefits of being exposed to pleasant sensory stimulation out of doors, such as the countryside or seaside.

Pets can reduce the stress of loneliness for lonely people. Just as being touched can be relaxing, so can petting an animal. Paro is an interactive robot in the form of a baby seal. It is designed to be a substitute for a live animal in hospitals and care settings – it is very strokable – and it is designed to respond in a way that is appealing to its owner.

Going on holiday is one of the stressors listed by Holmes and Rahe (see Chapter 2). However, although there is undoubtedly a stressful element to going on holiday – waiting at an airport is often stressful – holidays can also provide many opportunities for relaxation. To repeat what was said in Chapter 2, if the uncertainties of the trip can be reduced, then a holiday can be a valuable way of moving out of a stressful repetitive routine. Despite the potential stress of travel and despite the stress of uncertainty, the overall effect of going on holiday *can* be relaxing and health promoting.

Just because something is enjoyed does not guarantee that it is relaxing. Something that is enjoyable can also be stressful. Watching television is enjoyable, but one consistent finding is that the length of time spent watching is correlated with depression and poor mood. It may be that long hours in front of the television reduce physical activity and it is the lack of physical activity that is responsible for the depression. It may be that depressed people watch more television. However, the fact remains that television watching is not relaxing. On the contrary, research shows that when people watch violent or horrific scenes, their bodies respond with almost the same autonomic arousal that would occur if they experienced or watched those scenes in real life. Enjoyment is not a good guide to relaxation.

Summary

The adverse effects of *chronic* stress can be mitigated to a large degree through the use of techniques that produce a relaxation response. These techniques need to be practised over an extended period for them to be effective. Chronic stress is counteracted by chronic relaxation. Rather than considering what is the most successful technique, a more sensible way of thinking is to ask, 'What is the most successful technique for whom?' Stress-busting techniques work only if they are the techniques the individual prefers and practises regularly.

This 100 ideas section gives ways you can explore the subject in more depth. It's much more than just the usual reading list.

100 IDEAS

Five introductions to the wider topic of health psychology

1 Ogden, J., *Health Psychology: A Textbook* (McGraw-Hill International, 2012).

2 Morrison, V., and Bennett, P., *An Introduction to Health Psychology* (Pearson Education, 2009).

3 Marks, D. F., Murray, M., Evans, B., and Vida Estacio, E., *Health Psychology: Research and Practice* (Sage, 2011).

4 Taylor, S., *Health Psychology* (McGraw-Hill, 2009).

5 Lyon, A. C., and Chamberlain, K., *Health Psychology: A Critical Introduction* (Cambridge University Press, 2006).

Five thought-provoking books

6 Kirsch, I., *The Emperor's New Drugs: Exploding the Anti-depressant Myth* (Random House, 2009). Tells the story that challenges the current use of antidepressants.

7 Wolfram, S., *A New Kind of Science* (Wolfram Media, 2002). Shows how living systems can result from the repetition of simple computer programs.

8 Schulkin, J., *Adaptation and Well-being: Social Allostasis* (Cambridge University Press, 2011). A detailed book showing how biological systems encode information.

9 Hyland, M.E., *The Origins of Health and Disease* (Cambridge University Press, 2011). A complex book showing how disease and functional disorders can be understood in terms of errors in the body's 'software programs'.

10 Lipton, B., *The Biology of Belief: Unleashing the Power of Consciousness, Matter and Miracles* (Cygnus Books, 2005). An easy-to-read book linking biology and beliefs.

Three questionnaires that can be downloaded from the Internet

11 For measuring personality: The Big Five Inventory. See: http://www.ocf.berkeley.edu/~johnlab/bfi.htm

12 Scales for measuring mood: The positive and negative mood scale, expanded form, or PANAS-X. See http://www2.psychology.uiowa.edu/faculty/clark/panas-x.pdf

13 For measuring life satisfaction: Satisfaction with Life Scale. See: http://internal.psychology.illinois.edu/~ediener/SWLS.html

Ten proverbs

All countries have proverbs that provide advice about how to live a stress-free life:

14 All work and no play makes Jack a dull boy.

15 Better a lean peace than a fat victory.

16 A friend in need is a friend indeed.

17 A soft answer turns away wrath.

18 A wise man changes his mind, a fool never will.

19 A heavy purse makes a light heart.

20 Politeness costs little, but yields much.

21 Money is a good servant but a bad master.

22 If you try to please all, you please none.

23 Every cloud has a silver lining.

Five scales for measuring stress

Several questionnaires that are useful for measuring stress can be downloaded from the Internet. Here are some examples that are well regarded.

24 **Self-report scales that measure stress indirectly (see Chapter 7):**
Search the Internet (for example, using Google) for 'Cardiff stress questionnaire'.

25 **A quick questionnaire from Sue Firth:**
Search the Internet for 'Sue Firth stress questionnaire'.

26 **Bradford University stress questionnaire, particularly useful for students:**
Search the Internet for 'Bradford stress questionnaire'.

27 **The Glazer stress control questionnaire (also gives an indicator of Type A versus Type B personality):**
Search the Internet for 'Glazer stress control lifestyle questionnaire'.

28 **A longer stress questionnaire:**
Search the Internet for 'NHS stress questionnaire'.

Five misconceptions about stress

29 Stress is all in the mind.

30 If you enjoy doing something, you can't be stressed.

31 Stress affects other people, not me.

32 Babies are too young to experience stress.

33 Stress-related illness isn't proper illness.

Ten common signs that someone is experiencing chronic stress

34 Frequent headaches

35 Difficulty getting to sleep

36 Waking up too early in the morning

37 Dizziness

38 Irritability

39 Stomach problems – constipation, diarrhoea, pain

40 Fatigue for no reason

41 Twitch in eye or other part of the body

42 Racing heart

43 Frequent colds or sore throats

Four books that provide information about stress-free utopias – though not to everyone's taste

44 B. F Skinner, *Walden Two*. First published 1948 (Hackett Publishing Company, 2005)

45 Huxley, A., *Brave New World*. First published 1932 (Vintage, 2007)

46 More, T., *Utopia*. First published 1516 (Cambridge University Press, 2002)

47 Carey, J. (ed.), *The Faber Book of Utopias* (Faber and Faber, 1999)

Three responsibilities of employers

48 Monitor factors that might indicate high levels of stress – such as absenteeism, high staff turnover, staff conflict and indicators of dissatisfaction.

49 Make sure that health and safety policies that address stress are in place and that risk assessment is carried out regularly.

50 Plan for stress-related risk when significant organizational change takes place.

Three quotes from Hans Selye, stress pioneer

51 'Every stress leaves an indelible scar, and the organism pays for its survival after a stressful situation by becoming a little older.'

52 'As much as we thirst for approval, we dread condemnation.'

53 'Chance is a lady who smiles only upon those few who know how to make her smile.'

Seven research articles on stress and disease that are open access – though not always easy to read

54 Stress and the immune system:
http://www.ncbi.nlm.nih.gov/pmc/articles/PMC1361287/

55 Psychological stress and disease:
Search the Internet for 'Cohen psychological stress and disease'.

56 Stress and asthma:
http://www.ncbi.nlm.nih.gov/pmc/articles/PMC3052958/

57 Stress in the womb and life expectancy:
http://www.pnas.org/content/108/33/E513.full

58 Stress in childhood and disease:
http://www.ncbi.nlm.nih.gov/pmc/articles/PMC3402030/

59 Stress over the lifespan:
Search the Internet for 'lupien effects of stress throughout the lifespan on the brain, behaviour and cognition'.

60 Stress as a cause of obesity:
Search the Internet for 'Dallman stress-induced obesity and the emotional nervous system'.

Five things managers, board members and CEOs need to know

61 Employers have a legal duty of care towards their employees. Care includes protecting them from biological and psychological stress.

62 Employers should understand and champion actions to reduce stress.

63 Employers should recognize the signs of stress (including absenteeism and illness) and identify the causes rather than focusing on symptoms.

64 The relevant UK government website is http://www.hse.gov.uk/stress/furtheradvice/legalresponsibility.htm

65 Several websites are provided by the US government, including:
https://www.osha.gov/SLTC/emergencypreparedness/resilience_resources/support_documents/supervisorintra/intradeployment_supervisors.html

Ten sources of information for mental relaxation techniques

66 Kabat-Zinn, J. *Wherever You Go, There You Are* (New York: Hyperion, 2005). Easy-to-read book on mindfulness.

67 Langer, E.J. *Mindfulness* (Boston: Addison-Wesley/ Addison Wesley Longman, 1989). Easy-to-read book on mindfulness.

68 It is possible to pay **for online mindfulness courses**, but many are free. Search online. For example: http://www.freemindfulness.org/

69 This is probably the most useful website of all. It provides a **variety of techniques** all for free and all from a respected US university: https://www.dartmouth.edu/~healthed/relax/downloads. html#deep

70 Details of how to conduct **self-compassion therapy** can be found at: http://www.self-compassion.org/

71 Search the Internet for 'acceptance and commitment therapy'.

72 A really useful website on **self-determination theory**, hosted by a US university. Provides access to the research literature as well as questionnaires and other forms of information: http://www.selfdeterminationtheory.org/

73 The website for **positive psychology**, hosted by a US university, provides useful information and techniques: http://www.ppc.sas.upenn.edu/

74 Search the Internet for 'laughter therapy' and have a look at some of the YouTube films.

75 **The Velten technique** is a method of enhancing mood by repeating positive framed words. Details available at: http://www.wellbeingwizard.com/index.php?option=com_ content&task=view&id=503&Itemid=98

Ten relaxing complementary and alternative therapies

Ten simple things to do or avoid to reduce stress

86 Set your alarm clock to wake you 10 minutes earlier and go to bed 15 minutes earlier. You will be less rushed in the morning and start the day less stressed.

87 Be kind to yourself! Treats are not a luxury. They are a necessary part of life. Give yourself treats. Find what you enjoy and do it.

88 Make sure that you find some time during the day for relaxation. Spend time 'being' rather than 'doing'.

89 Don't rush around searching for something that cannot be found!

90 Look for a silver lining in difficult situations.

91 If something or someone annoys you, control your emotions before acting or speaking. Do not be ruled by anger.

92 Learn how to say no. Saying no is essential for avoiding stress.

93 Let go of the past. Look to the future. Don't blame yourself.

94 Spend time with people who make you feel good. Choose your friends; don't be ruled by others' choices. If you are a dolphin, then swim with the dolphins. Don't swim with the sharks.

95 Do not seek perfection in everything – learn how to compromise.

Two videos providing information about t'ai chi/qigong

There are a large number of videos online for t'ai chi/qigong and for yoga, not always well produced. Here are two that are worth trying:

96 http://www.youtube.com/watch?v=PNtWqDxwwMg

97 http://www.youtube.com/watch?v=EaEZVfhn07o

Three unsolved scientific problems

98 What is the cause of functional disorders (such as ME/CFS, fibromyalgia and irritable bowel syndrome)? Functional disorders are common, but despite years of investigation a biological explanation has not been discovered. To say that it is 'just psychological' is misleading, because minds do not occur without bodies.

99 What forms of lifestyle modification can best undo the effects of stress-related problems, including functional disorders?

100 To what extent can pharmacological interventions help in stress-related disorders?

Index

All That Matters books are written by the world's leading experts, to introduce the most exciting and relevant areas of an important topic to students and general readers.

From Bioethics to Muhammad and Philosophy to Sustainability, the *All That Matters* series covers the most controversial and engaging topics from science, philosophy, history, religion and other fields. The authors are world-class academics or top public intellectuals, on a mission to bring the most interesting and challenging areas of their subject to new readers.

Each book contains a unique '100 ideas' section, giving inspiration to readers whose interest has been piqued and who want to explore the subject further.